The Costs and Benefits of Deferred Giving

The
Costs and Benefits
of
Deferred Giving

Norman S. Fink
Howard C. Metzler

Prepared for the
Lilly Endowment, Inc.

Columbia University Press
New York   1982

Library of Congress Cataloging in Publication Data

Fink, Norman S., 1926–
The costs and benefits of deferred giving.

Bibliography: p.
Includes index.
1. Fund raising—United States.   2. Deferred giving
—United States—Cost effectiveness.   I. Metzler,
Howard C., 1924–   .   II. Title.
HV41.F46   658.1′522   81-21565
ISBN 0-231-05478-5   AACR2

Columbia University Press
New York   Guildford, Surrey

Clothbound editions of Columbia University Press books
are Smyth-sewn and printed on permanent and durable
acid-free paper.

Contents

Foreword

For many years, much of the nonprofit sector seemed to resist the introduction of such modern business practices as cost accounting, benefit analysis, econometric forecasting, actuarial projections, and risk investment. Many of the sector's decision makers wanted no part of concepts that seemed foreign to the long and honorable tradition of charitable giving in America.

In this tradition, givers are motivated by the noblest instincts, institutions scrupulously comply with the giver's wishes, and the work of charity is more of a calling than a career.

The tradition served the nonprofit sector during an extended period of accomplishment and there seemed to be every reason for optimism about the future of the sector and its institutions. Then inflation and other forces began to make themselves felt. Despite the tremendous achievements of American philanthropy, it suddenly was apparent that many nonprofit institutions were in a battle for survival.

We at the Lilly Endowment cannot claim to be the first to recognize the existence of this threat. However, our grant-making experience has taught us that not all institutions are doing all they can to broaden their base of support. Not all institutions are prepared to utilize the systematic fundraising techniques called for by today's economic and social climate.

So in the early 1970s, the Endowment began to provide limited support for projects designed to upgrade the fundraising activities of selected institutions. Our emphasis was on increased professionalism, on programs that sought to improve the skills of the development officers.

One phase of this effort involved planned or deferred giving. To gain information on this vital aspect of fundraising, the Endowment assisted in financing a thorough study of deferred giving at Pomona College. The pioneering deferred giving program developed by this California liberal arts school long has been considered one of the most advanced in the country.

As the study progressed, it became evident that the methods used by Pomona to determine costs and benefits could be adapted to the use of many other nonprofit institutions. Indeed, the study has so many significant, practical applications that a decision was made to seek publication in book form.

The pages that follow are a result of that decision. We believe they offer innovative ideas to all nonprofit institutions which desire not only to be accountable to their benefactors but also to be efficient with their resources.

We join all those who made this report possible in the belief that it will help institutions improve their fundraising through effective planned giving programs. That, in turn, will constitute an important contribution to the strengthening of American philanthropy and the nonprofit institutions it exists to serve.

Lilly Endowment, Inc.   Thomas H. Lake
Indianapolis, Indiana   *Chairman of the Board*
                                         and President

Preface

Too many colleges and universities and their sister tax-exempt institutions continue to seek resources in ancient, honorable, and traditional ways while the methods of charitable giving and the effective promotion of them have reached new levels of sophistication. Our colleges teach the concepts of management, marketing, and economics and have done so for many decades, but many of our institutions of higher education naively ignore these working tools in their approach to the private sector for gifts.

The demand for accountability of institutions serving the public good can no longer be satisfied with self-serving platitudes. Life in the 1980s is characterized by technological complexity, and we are committed to the training of high-talent manpower to accommodate the needs of the times. The rapid rate of innovation and change has not overlooked the charitable institutions of the United States, but rarely, at least in the critical area of fundraising, have they developed the capacity to adjust to these changed circumstances.

On February 19, 1981, the *New York Times* reported: THE $10,000-A-YEAR COLLEGE EDUCATION HAS ARRIVED. Tuition, room, and board per academic year for 1981–1982 will exceed $10,000 at "such pace-setting schools as Harvard, Yale, Brown, Bennington, Columbia, and M.I.T." At Princeton the price tag will be $9,994; at Brandeis, $9,824; and at Pomona, $9,122.

With these rates increasing at a faster rate than inflation, the need for increased scholarship and fellowship aid will be critical if private colleges and universities are to continue to compete for the quality student irrespective of financial capacity to pay these charges.

At the same time, President Reagan, in the presentation of his administration's economic program on February 18, 1981, made it clear that the nation is to receive shock therapy. Columnist Joseph Kraft reported in the *Boston Globe* of February 19, 1981:

> The theory behind the shock is the theory of inflationary expectations. The premise is that the chief force behind the ever-rising prices is the expectation by workers and businessmen and consumers that prices will keep on rising. The Reagan program (reducing income taxes, federal spending, federal regulation) is designed to break that expectation. Once the expectation is shattered, the theory goes, consumers will start saving, funds will become available for investment, long-term interest rates will fall and the economy will regenerate itself in a burst of new activity, new growth and higher productivity.

While it is much too early to forecast the specific economic consequences of this program as it relates to higher education and charitable enterprises, there can be little doubt that appropriations, relied on in the past, will be cut. Financial aid programs underwritten by Congress will be pared as will funds supporting government grants to the arts and humanities.

In an article entitled "Rites of Passage, from the Tripod to the Waterbed of Philanthropy," which appeared in *CASE Currents* in 1977 I wrote:

> According to anthropologists, every society signifies the coming of age of its members by ceremony (rites of passage, if you will). For the society of fundraisers, the three-legged stool or tripod of giving (annual, capital, and deferred) has been basic to the training of the novitiate. Charitable giving has undergone a crucial metamorphosis since 1969 and now the ceremony is over. Accordingly, in 1977, for the reasons which follow, the tripod must give way. The three legs must be dismembered from the seat.
>
> With the "waste not, want not" admonition of our predecessors in mind, it is time for development officers to come of age and to redesign the parts of the tripod into a new and mature characterization—a waterbed, perhaps. No longer do annual, capital, and planned giving conveniently fit into that traditional tripartite mold. Today they must

blend and flow to adjust to the donor's configuration of assets, income, obligations, and estate.

To perpetuate the third leg of the tripod—bequests and deferred or planned giving—as a separate and distinct source of financial support is equally anachronistic. Few major development campaigns for substantial support in 1977 and hereafter will succeed within the boundaries of that old-time religion.

Seeking a major philanthropic commitment from an individual today requires considerations commensurate with the times. How best can that commitment be realized? Chances are, the only way to the aspired gift is through a combination of gift-giving methods. All types of giving become relevant. "Gift objective" should today become the password to replace "dollar goal." (pp. 8–9)

Major successful capital fundraising campaigns, completed since the writing of that article, including the $255 million campaign at the University of Pennsylvania, in which I was privileged to participate, have validated the waterbed concept. Thirty to forty percent of the campaign gifts received from individuals were planned or deferred gifts. Experience at Stanford, Notre Dame, and elsewhere has been similar.

In the series published under the title New Directions for Institutional Advancement, a booklet (volume 3) edited by Warren Heemann was entitled *Analyzing the Cost Effectiveness of Fund Raising*. In that very useful booklet, Richard J. Ramsden reported on "The COFHE (Consortium on Financing Higher Education) Development Study." This study was undertaken in 1976 by a group of twenty-five colleges and universities of which Pomona College and the University of Pennsylvania were two. Fourteen universities and eleven colleges participated and in 1976 these institutions raised approximately $400 million in private gifts, about one sixth of all funds raised by colleges and universities in that year. The study covered many aspects of the development programs of each of the institutions, but a key question to which it was addressed was the allocation of development resources. As was stated by Joel P. Smith in the foreword to that study:

We need to study costs in order to understand better what to spend money on . . . which expenditures cause which results and why? It would be vain to assume that we shall ever answer that question completely. Serendipity will always be an aspect of our work. So-phisticated hunches will remain a respectful method of reaching decisions. But granting that the question cannot be answered completely, we can work on it. And to the extent that we are able to refine our understanding of the relationships between resources and results, our fund raising and university relations program will become, by degree, more rational and—this is the cardinal point—more productive.

The details of the study can be reviewed in Ramsden's article but for purposes of this report, note should be made of the recognition by that study that development results often reflect the influence in efforts over long periods of time and therefore, although detailed expenditure data could only be obtained for a single year—comparing results and efforts must be done with caution. It was nonetheless deemed useful to compare development expenses as they existed in 1976 with average gift support over the prior decade, the three years 1973–1975 and the year 1976. As a percentage of annual private gift support, development expenses in 1975–1976 averaged approximately 7 percent at the fourteen universities and 11 percent at the eleven colleges. When university relations expenses were added, the percentages rose to approximately 11 percent and 19 percent, respectively. Perhaps one of the most significant conclusions was: "Finally, considering that almost half of almost all gifts from individuals are in the form of bequests or deferred gifts, few institutions appeared to be devoting sufficient resources to this endeavor, especially compared with the resources devoted to the obtaining of currently expendable gifts."

Bear in mind this report was issued in 1976. Since then the development efforts at these institutions have changed markedly.

The study found that gifts by individuals accounted for almost three-quarters of the support of the colleges and 56 percent of the support of the universities over the decade 1966–1975. This is somewhat less than for all charitable institutions but still represents a very significant proportion of resource. For universities, approximately 38 percent of the support from individuals came by way of bequests and 8 percent in various deferred gift forms while 54 percent were outright gifts by living individuals. In the case of the eleven colleges, the comparable figures were 35, 10, and 55 percent.

In the twenty-fifth anniversary issue of *Giving USA*, a compilation of facts and trends on American philanthropy for the year 1979, it is reported that Americans contributed an unprecedented total of $43.31 billion to charitable causes. About 90 percent of this was given by individuals, in the form of outright gifts, deferred gifts, and bequests. This new record total represented an increase of 11.4 percent from the $39.56 billion contributed in 1978. For comparison purposes, sales of General Motors in 1979 amounted to $66 billion and IBM had sales of $22.9 billion.

Ramsden goes on to cite the notable differences among the COFHE institutions in terms of effort, allocation of resources, and results. In the case of many of the colleges, little or nothing was received in deferred gifts and at a number of schools there were no deferred gift programs at that time. Pomona College, on the other hand, was at the outside extreme of the study since 56 percent of its gifts from individuals were received in the deferred gift category for the year studied.

No effort was made in that study to determine the present value of gifts of future interests but the study concluded with a plea which has not gone unheard. Mr. Ramsden said: "Given the critical role that private gift support must continue to play in higher education, it is hoped that the study was a beginning that others will be encouraged to pursue and develop in the years ahead."

The heretofore unanswered questions to which this study is directed are simple; the answers are not. Cost accounting and benefit analysis with respect to deferred gifts are explored here for the first time. The traditional measurement of cost per dollar received does not address the economic and financial complexities of charitable gifts subject to a life or term of years. Like the pledge, the charitable remainder interest may be explicit as to amount of gift for campaign counting purposes, but the true value of that gift episode, that charitable commitment, at the time it happens, is a guess. The net value of such gifts are affected by cost of acquisition; the cost of management in the case of a life income trust is a second factor—and, as the text will show, they are relatively low and ascertainable. Where risk enters the picture, the value will perceptibly and progressively decline commensurate with the length of time between the date that gift agreement is signed and the date on which the charity receives cash or property for its own use. Risk has been approached in this study on three key levels—investments, actuarial experience, and economic prediction. With this knowledge, a modernized development program can be financed with a rationale for the true return on that investment that has not been available. With this knowledge, realistic criteria of acceptance for deferred gifts can be established on a basis that has not been available, and some new and pragmatic thinking can be applied to the allocation of institutional fund raising resources to personnel and program.

As early as 1977 when work started on this study at Pomona College, we were uncertain as to what paths might be chosen, but not the destination. Without precedent to follow, the gracious support of Pomona College and the Lilly Endowment permitted a research exercise upon which this report is based. The objectives, variously stated, included the use of modern financial and economic methodology, the application of as good a program of experience in deferred giving as existed anywhere, and an effort to provide a formula for the determination of all the costs of a deferred gift program and to provide an analysis of the benefits relating to those costs. All of this to permit charitable institutions to respond accurately and courageously to demands for accountability and to improve and enhance their fundraising programs so necessary to future viability and solvency. As this is being written, the "future shock" continues and forecasting economic conclusions remains as much in the realm of Merlin the Magician as it is the agenda of econometricians. It is the hope of all those who have had a part in this study that this will be a beginning.

Norman S. Fink

The Costs and Benefits of Deferred Giving

Introduction

In the organization of this report the primary consideration has been how to make the results useful to the community of charitable institutions to whom deferred or planned giving programs of fundraising are or may be significant. A second goal is to simplify what was discovered to be a complex task and to express the conclusions in understandable prose that would have meaning to all who might undertake to read this report, whether trustee or treasurer, president or development officer.

The Pomona Plan is explored in depth in the Ernst & Whinney report appended hereto. Initially, William B. Dunseth served as co-director of the study and assumed the leadership role in guiding the efforts of the Ernst & Whinney team of analysts. Dunseth, now retired from his position as Vice President for Development at Pomona College, found it necessary for reasons of health to give up his responsibilities for co-supervision of the study. He recommended that Howard Metzler, whom he had personally trained to be his successor as Director of the Pomona Annuity and Trust Program, be named as an additional co-director to take on these duties. Without Bill Dunseth's foresight and determination this report would not have been written.

The Ernst & Whinney Report represents over two years of combined effort of teams of representatives of Ernst & Whinney under the supervision of Jerry Walker and Dan Freeman, with faculty, staff, and students of Pomona College, helpful econometricians from a variety of institutions, and the authors of this report. The challenge to explore new ground in this research would not have succeeded without the encouragement and cooperation of President David Alexander, Vice President and Treasurer Frederick F. Moon of Pomona College, and Charles A. Johnson, Special Consultant to the Lilly Endowment. The administrative assistance of Mrs. Terry Timko of the Pomona College staff was especially valuable in preparing the manuscript.

As the study progressed, it appeared necessary to expand the final report to include a broad based background and approach. This is not intended to be a how-to-do-it manual or an authoritative treatise on the whole subject. What follows is a pragmatic report designed to establish standards by which charitable institutions can maximize, to the extent possible, the true benefits from gifts whose ultimate use by the institution is deferred.

The text is divided into ten chapters, the first of which places planned and deferred giving programs in appropriate context. The second chapter is a statement of the problem to be solved, followed by the solution expressed in general terms. (The specific findings which relate exclusively to the Pomona Plan, from which all conclusions derive, are treated in the summary analysis of the Ernst & Whinney Report; see chapter 6.)

Chapter 3 describes the origin of the Pomona Plan, its history, and composition. Chapters 4 and 5 detail Pomona College's marketing of its annuity and trust program and the steps leading up to this study. Other approaches to cost-benefit analysis of fundraising are reviewed. None, however, grapple with the thorny questions posed by the special nature of determining "the present value of a future gift interest, the realization and use of which is deferred either for a term of years or a period measured by lives in being."

Chapter 6 deals with Pomona College only and summarizes the methods employed and findings ascertained in the joint effort of the authors and representatives of Ernst & Whinney. Efforts to test these methods with data from other institutions are described thereafter. The Ernst & Whinney Report, see appendix A, spells out the particularity of the approach to the results.

With the assistance of Harry A. Turner of Stanford University, a method for evaluating the criteria for acceptability of deferred gifts and a rationale therefore is set forth in chapter 8. The management of life income gifts and annuities, which becomes even more significant than gift development in a cost-benefit analysis, serves as the subject of chapter 9. Each institution will face policy issues in determining its course and the final chapter offers some conclusions and recommendations.

Evolution rather than inspiration better characterizes the process by which this report has been completed. What has been learned by the authors is perhaps best expressed by a quotation of Louis D. Brandeis: "One cannot be pulled up a great height. Only a short distance can you be lifted by your arms. But in climbing with your feet and stepping on the solid ground below, you can climb mountains." (Mason, *Brandeis*, p. 61).

There is no doubt that gift returns from a combined financial and planned gift development program that is well-conceived and efficiently managed will be rewarding and economically beneficial. What follows is a statement and rationale demonstrating that thesis and signaling the hazards that must be overcome to achieve a favorable institutional result.

Planned and Deferred Giving Programs

Don't leave home without it.

To many fundraisers, the term "deferred giving" refers to all gifts *except* those that are physically passed, like a football, from the hand of the giver to the hand of the receiver. In deferred gifts, there can be short and long passes, even laterals and end around plays. However, bequests, insurance policy gifts, life income trusts, pooled income fund gifts, charitable gift annuities, and remainder interests in farms and homes seldom pass simply and quickly from the giver to the receiver.

Preferred is the term "planned giving" to "deferred giving." Judge Learned Hand once said: "Words are not only the keys of persuasion but the triggers of action." Indeed, the institution's enjoyment of a charitable gift may be deferred, but when a donor transfers securities to fund a charitable remainder unitrust or annuity, he or she has made a *present transfer.* This is a gift—even though the donor's life and that of some other person or persons—a spouse, parent, or child—represent the institution's waiting period. Such a gift is irrevocable, unlike a provision in a will, which can be revoked by rewriting.

Nonetheless, even in the case of a bequest, which could be changed or dropped, it is not uncommon to hear a contributor to a charitable institution say, "I have provided for the university in my will." In the donor's mind—at least nine times out of ten—the gift has been made, and it ill behooves one to suggest otherwise. Experience suggests most wills are not changed and designated legacies to charity tend to be repeated even where changes are made.

A gift often expresses one person's relationship to another person or institution. Because people express themselves in different ways and because financial circumstances differ, it is essential for colleges, universities, and other institutions that rely on charitable gifts to have available different gift options for their donors. The broad planned giving option embraces many different methods from which the donor and his legal adviser may choose with the assistance of a skilled university representative.

It is taking time to realize and develop the potential of this category of giving. This cost-benefit analysis, coming over a decade after the Tax Reform Act of 1969, illustrates the fact that the state of the art is still to be developed and refined. It is, after all, more complex to complete a charitable gift remainder arrangement than to accept a check. To understand the current status of planned giving, it might be helpful to look back to 1960 and use the University of Pennsylvania as an example.

It was then that the bequest and deferred gift program started at Penn in a modest way, although such gifts were received even in colonial times. In the 1960s, many people considered a discussion of bequests to be unseemly or even macabre. Accordingly, a simple brochure was mailed reciting recent testamentary gifts to the university to senior alumni and friends. The brochure was sponsored by a committee of distinguished alumni—most of them members of the bar.

As time went on, it became clear that bequests represented the principal source of gifts to the university's endowment. Volunteer class bequest counselors were organized and the unspoken became the spoken. The university, through these class counselors, asked alumni to remember Pennsylvania in their estate plans. A number did—and told the university about it. The growth of that precious group of farsighted philanthropists became a continuing goal.

An important milestone in this chronology is the Tax Reform Act of 1969. For the first time, a federal statute spelled out the ways in which charitable remainder life income trusts could be established so as to qualify for tax deductions. Prior to 1969, institutions relied on revenue rulings which cannot be relied upon by nonparties to the specific ruling. Congress created substantial income, gift, and estate tax incentives for individuals who placed support for the university high among their social priorities. Particularly, the statute made it possible to provide such support while retaining a life income—to receive a present income tax deduction while avoiding tax liabilities such as tax on long-term capital gains.

With the opening of these new legislative vistas and during the two-year wait for the necessary IRS regulations, it became clear that those persons who had already decided to do something for Penn in their estate plans were natural prospects for life income trust gifts. They had made the commitment to give, and now, all that was necessary was to decide and persuade donors to adopt the best method to implement that important decision.

Since 1969, it has become increasingly clear that major capital gifts are more likely to be realized where the prospect has received information on charitable remainder life income gifts by way of cultivation. Such methods of giving are the tools by which large gifts can be made larger, reluctant prospects can become satisfied donor/investors, one-time givers can become annual repeaters, and the fine art of estate planning can be an imaginative resource for future support.

This is why planned giving or deferred giving can no longer be treated as a nonpriority program in development offices. Charitable institutions cannot afford to ignore these programs with the rationalization that what is needed are "current gifts."

In working with a donor (and his or her advisers) to produce a substantial commitment, the representative of a philanthropic organization must provide proper advice that reflects the mutual intent of the donor and the charity, and must demonstrate how this intent can best be realized. Federal and state income and estate tax incentives to charitable giving alone may not provide the best guidelines of how much and what should be given. Consideration of an individual's tax status ought to be augmented by a broad view of the family and individual economic circumstances, so that combinations of situations and available deductions can be considered in framing an overall plan for the gift objective.

The scheduling of payments on a major commitment to philanthropy may well be determined by the review of such data and consideration. Attention might be directed to the use of periodic payments (sometimes called "annual giving"), infrequent but substantial payments (sometimes called "capital giving"), and charitable life income trust gifts (sometimes called "deferred gifts"). All, if need be, are relevant and could be backed by a testamentary make-up provision to prevent the possibility that a premature death would defeat the achievement of a gift objective.

The successful development effort in today's economic climate must not only be well planned in the traditional sense but also take into account alternative and sophisticated methods of giving. As a prerequisite to success, it is essential that all participants in the fundraising scenario, from the trustee to the telethonist, from the president to the petitioner, from the savant to the solicitor, know and understand the significance of all forms of giving. They need not be specialists or technicians, but generalists able to communicate the notion that a planned gift is superior and of more value than a spontaneous gift, both to the donor and to the donee.

Professionalism is today's hallmark of successful fundraising. In discerning appropriate threshold criteria of useful deferred giving through a cost-benefit analysis, an institution is acting with prudence and a donor will understand and approve such an approach.

The key to a successful life income trust and annuity program is thorough and careful preparation. It was Oliver Wendell Holmes who said: "Every calling is great when greatly pursued." Bringing a life income trust or gift annuity to fruition may take several years and rarely less than twelve months, during which time cultivation of that donor is "greatly pursued." The fact that a major planned gift usually requires years of consistent cultivation means this is no business for the transient. Indeed, it is an ideal calling for an emeritus college president or retired dean.

Once careful cultivation results in an agreement, that is only the beginning. Such agreements involve lifetime contact with the beneficiary and later in this report the nature and extent of the management and performance of that agreement will be dealt with in detail.

In accepting charitable remainder life income trust gifts, a charity undertakes a commitment as a fiduciary. Annuities are based on contractual obligations. From the common-law traditions of the seventeenth century to modern precedents, the responsibilities of a fiduciary are uncompromising: full disclosure, complete fairness, and reasonable prudence. The leaders of the institution must understand the commitment that such a program demands; they must be willing to proceed not as spectators but as energetic participants.

Commitment must start with the governing board. Its members must want this program. They must understand that in time and properly mounted, such a program will produce assets that will enable them to plan for the future with confidence. The determination of the value of those assets is the subject of this report. Each reader will have to examine his own institutional policies in order to justify such confidence. They must show the determination to make the investment in the future *now*. To make the program a success, the trustees or regents must act aggressively to identify deferred gift prospects, provide adequate staff, and supply the resources for a full and effective program.

To succeed, a planned giving program should incorporate the following considerations:

The institution must gain rather than lose from contributions in the form of charitable remainder life income gifts or annuities but by the same token, risks must be undertaken with courage where certainty may be elusive.

The institution should periodically evaluate its life income gift and annuity program to assure that the advantages to the institution outweigh the disadvantages.

The institutional development program should include a range of methods of giving, encouraged by tax incentives, so that its donors have options available to fit their circumstances.

Because new methods of giving require new methods of preparation, solicitation, and management, the institution and its staff must be alert to respond to changing laws and circumstances.

The institution's fundraising officers, its lawyers, and those charged with the management and disposition of these funds must coordinate their efforts and communicate continuously and constructively.

The institution must draw up sanguine and productive guidelines for its planned giving program; however, they should be flexible enough to accommodate special situations. A separate treatment of this concept appears in chapter 8.

The institution's stewardship in managing the planned giving program should be of a quality that will encourage repeat gifts.

All known legal risks that could lead to wrongful liability must be overcome in the negotiation and execution of life income gift agreements (e.g., improperly drawn instruments).

Responsibilities and authority must be defined and delineated to permit prompt and efficient decision making.

In the fall of 1980, the following appeared in the Northwest Area Foundation (NAF) Newsletter:

> Deferred giving programs have become the subject of enormous interest for colleges, universities, and charitable organizations in recent years. It is important that any organization contemplating a major commitment to deferred giving as a part of its resource development effort understand the implications of the program. Failure to do so may be the difference between deferred gifts being a bane or a blessing. It could bring administrative problems, exposure to litigation, and more liabilities than solution to the financial future of the institution.
>
> A deferred gifts program involves institutional commitment extending far into the future in terms of governing board responsibilities, central administration support, and donor relations. Tax, legal, and financial management implications related to administration of an effective deferred gifts program must be carefully defined and understood. A deferred giving program can be a very significant means of undergirding your institution's financial future.

It may be repetitive but it is certainly worth emphasizing.

A dramatic illustration of the significance of planned giving programs carefully and professionally orchestrated is found in the splendid work of the Northwest Area Foundation.

It created and supported a self-help incentive program with a group of small selected independent colleges in northwest America that were facing grave financial problems. Eighteen colleges were selected in 1974 and grants were made to provide them with the expertise and the trained staff to obtain and manage deferred gifts—an otherwise unknown method of fundraising in these schools. Five years later, twelve of the eighteen schools reported approximately $59 million of confirmed deferred gifts. The present value of those gifts in constant dollars should be determinable by those institutions if they choose to use the lessons of this report.

Among several other articles on the topic of planned giving which appeared in the November 1979 issue of CASE Currents, published by the Council for Advancement and Support of Education, there was an article by Harvey Devries and Karen Grabow which grew out of their work for the Northwest Area Foundation and was directed to the question of the employment and retention of planned giving officers. In two charts, they provide an excellent insight into the kind of people institutions need in this arena as well as a useful job description. In this cost-benefit analysis the single largest direct cost relates to personnel and accordingly, the data deserves a place in this review of planned giving programs.

Chart 1. Major Categories of Job Performance—Deferred Gifts Officer

The successful deferred gifts officer:

1. *Keeps up-to-date.* Stays abreast of legal and technical developments in estate planning and charitable donations through workshops, seminars, conferences, and publications; remains conversant with developments in education in general as well as with the goals, programs, and trends within his or her own institution.
2. *Provides general information on estate planning.* Initiates regular informational mailings to alumni and other friends of the institution; responds to inquiries; speaks to interested groups.
3. *Identifies prospective donors.* Determines where to spend time to the best advantage; researches respondents to mailings or those

who come to the deferred gifts officer's attention through referrals or direct inquiry. Maintains an effective records system and an efficient follow-up procedure to ensure that all contacts receive appropriate attention.

4. *Develops the prospect's interest and commitment.* Patiently but persistently cultivates the prospect through correspondence or personal visits by the deferred gifts officer or others (volunteers may be helpful). Answers the prospect's questions, keeping the prospect mindful of the college and its programs; gains the prospect's friendship and trust.

5. *Determines feasibility of various contribution options.* Elicits information about the prospect's assets and needs and chooses the most appropriate option available; considers the deferred gifts program as a part of the total development picture and remains open to the possibility of current as well as deferred gifts.

6. *Writes the proposal.* Commits the plan to paper in a manner that is both convincing and understandable to the prospect and the prospect's agents; frequently consults with experts to work out details.

7. *Closes.* Discusses, clarifies, and perhaps modifies the plan to meet the prospect's approval; gains the prospect's endorsement.

8. *Ensures that arrangements are properly executed.* Oversees and initiates arrangements through the proper channels (attorneys, trust departments, the college business office, etc.) and communicates with the prospect about them.

9. *Maintains the commitment of the donor.* Ensures that the donor retains confidence in the college and in the wisdom of the decision to make a deferred gift; keeps the donor informed of developments affecting the institution or relevant to estate planning or charitable gifts; keeps the donor open to the possibility of repeat business or of referrals from the donor.

Chart 2. Profile: Behavioral Characteristics of Successful Deferred Gifts Officers

1. *Mental ability.* The ability to acquire and apply the requisite technical knowledge (i.e., a *conceptual* understanding of estate planning and tax laws); a facility with numbers; the ability to read and interpret government documents.

2. *Judgment and decision making.* The ability to think on one's feet; to evaluate relevant information, recognize alternatives, and reach logical conclusions based on the evidence at hand without

undue vacillation; to handle day-to-day problems in a practical and effective way.

3. *Planning and organizing*. The ability to structure personal activities (and sometimes the activities of others); to maximize productivity and efficiency; to arrange documentation and information in a systematic manner; to establish objective and measurable plans for accomplishment of goals; to set priorities.

4. *Oral communications skill*. The ability to use the spoken word effectively and to make oneself understood both in personal, informal settings, and before groups; to listen effectively so as to acquire and respond with relevant information; to project an image of credibility and sincerity in one's communication.

5. *Written communications skill*. The ability to get a written message across in a clear, direct, interesting, and effective manner.

6. *Human relations understanding and skill*. The ability to perceive and react sensitively to the needs and feelings of others; skill in developing relationships that enhance understanding, communication, and friendliness.

7. *Salesmanship*. Though there is no room for high pressure tactics, the ability to influence, persuade, motivate, and convince others *is* required.

8. *Achievement, motivation, and initiative*. The tendency to work in accordance with self-imposed work standards and discipline; to be a self-starter; willingness to devote extra effort to get a job done.

9. *Persistence*. Determination to continue to pursue objectives despite disappointments and rejections.

10. *Self-assurance*. Realistic faith in oneself and one's abilities; aplomb that commands the respect of others.

11. *Flexibility*. Ability to adapt and respond appropriately to the demands of various situations.

12. *Maturity*. Ability to delay immediate gratification and short-term rewards in order to achieve long-range goals; emotional and behavioral self-awareness; concern and consideration for the consequences of actions; ability to handle frustration and ambiguity constructively.

13. *Commitment*. Loyalty to one's organization and a belief in the value of education.

14. *Follow-through*. Skill in following up on commitments.

Other "must have" requirements include a bachelor's degree,

a willingness to travel, and an acceptable appearance. All those engaged in representing charitable institutions with prospective donors should, in addition, have finely tuned ethical standards which preclude unfairness, personal aggrandizement and, perhaps most important of all, which will prevent any jeopardy of his institution's credibility or integrity.

The Problem

A dollar is a dollar—or is it?

In early England only those of the crown and peerage could inherit property and many first sons, according to the record of early cases, were profligate. They were not inclined to wait respectfully upon the decease of their fathers and so they borrowed or sold their inheritances. Today, one can find classified advertisements in some newspapers by lenders or buyers soliciting such transactions. While lawyers for fathers and mothers were able to develop "spendthrift" clauses in trusts and wills to protect heirs against themselves, such transactions still take place. The question persists: how do the parties determine the present value of the future interest?

The same question can be asked of the pledge of a charitable gift over a period of time. A commitment, whether or not legally enforceable, to make a gift in installments over a period of years, involves a future interest. Usually made for a fixed dollar amount, the vicissitudes of the market place will determine what that same dollar will buy when it is received— and rarely will the real value be the same value as when pledged. The financial value and consequences of pledges, characteristically abundant in major capital fundraising campaigns and highly traditional among certain segments of the charitable community, is not the subject of this inquiry. Vincent A. Fulmer, then Vice President and Secretary of Massachusetts Institute of Technology, addressed the subject in an article in the *Harvard Business Review* in 1973. He advocated the need to discount the value of pledges in the context of prevailing interest rates.

Most college and university development programs now record "bequest expectancies" (i.e., persons who have advised that the institution is a beneficiary of their estate plans). Indeed some institutions such as Yale, Johns Hopkins, and Dartmouth include all or a portion of the value of expectancies in capital campaign totals. The rules of what is or is not to be included may be liberal or conservative. The relevant point is how does one evaluate such future interests. Such an inquiry is more complex with respect to charitable remainder trusts for the latter are irrevocable, while bequests are rarely so.

The common issue to all these transactions is the *determination of present value*. Valuing the charitable remainder gift in constant dollars, whether created by annuity agreement or trust indenture, is the core question of this study. To determine value, it is essential to know costs. The traditional measurement of cost per dollar of gift received does not address the economic complexities of deferred giving programs. The legislative push to regulate charitable fundraising through cost limitations must take into account the special nature of these gifts.

To start with, the period over which the costs of gift acquisition are incurred normally exceeds standard business time cycles. A single year, whether calendar or fiscal, is inadequate. The marketing process for deferred gifts is expected to take at least eighteen months from first contact to signed agreement and usually more. Frequently, it is impossible to attribute true costs because a casual alumni meeting on deferred gifts can plant a seed of interest that will bear fruit only five or ten years thereafter.

Costs in this study have been categorized into two segments, each of which normally extends well beyond a single year. They are: 1) the cultivation and solicitation costs incurred to obtain the agreement or outright bequest; and 2) the costs incurred to maintain and service the agreement as long as it is outstanding (see appendix A, E&W Report, section 3.2.2).

General observations which help establish the framework

for what follows include:

1. It is possible to estimate the cost–benefit ratio of a planned giving program.
2. This is a laborious task by any measure and initial attempts to simplify the estimation process proved unproductive.
3. A simpler process, derived from the cost–benefit analysis, is possible to permit the average charitable institution to analyze an existing planned giving program—or to decide to undertake a new program.
4. The cost effectiveness of the Pomona Plan, as herein described, showed a substantial return on investment (i.e., the total cost of operating the program).

NOTE: It should be noted that in analyzing the Pomona Plan, particularly unfavorable factors, some of which are not present in other college planned giving programs, are influential. First, marketing is predominately directed to non-alumni, which involves more individual cultivation and more competitive agreement terms and conditions. Second, erratic performance of the securities market together with high rates of inflation over the last decade (and more importantly forecasted for the future) created a difficult environment for managing deferred agreements. Third, Pomona's threshold gift acceptance criteria permitted agreements with young payees and for relatively small amounts.

5. The ultimate cost to obtain a dollar of benefit (measuring value at release time) was much higher than expected.
6. The cost of acquiring deferred gift agreements on a per dollar basis (the dollar valued at the signing of the agreement) falls into the expected range—10¢ or less on the dollar.
7. It is the continuing costs during the management period and the reduction in benefit value attributable to the years of deferral that combine to reduce the cost-benefit ratio.
8. On the out-of-pocket cost side, the use of assumptions in allocations of budget expenditures is not worrisome, for such costs tend to remain fixed at widely ranging operating levels notwithstanding the dollar volume of new agreements under management.
9. Record keeping for cost analysis is probably in reasonably good order at most institutions—though discretionary refinement consistent with financial policy of each institution may be necessary to cost account its deferred giving program.
10. The analysis of the benefits side is far more complicated than the costs side.

11. Record keeping as it relates to benefits is inadequate and unless preprogrammed elsewhere, will be difficult to capture or reconstruct.

12. The factors which make prediction imprecise in attempting to project the value of the remainder at the time an agreement is terminated are the inherent uncertainties in both actuarial estimates and econometric projections.

13. The most significant reduction in value (and therefore increase in cost) occurs in the process of discounting the future value of the remainder interest to its present value, i.e., the cost of having to wait, or, expressed another way, the capital opportunity cost.

An illustration of this concept of "present value" can be found in the treatment of an inquiry as to the present value of a matured pension plan. Murray Projector, a consulting actuary who has been most helpful to the authors of this report, has written the following in an article in *Family Advocate* (Summer 1979), p. 37 et seq.:

"We'll assume our subject is a 65-year-old male employee who has just retired and receives a $10,000 annual pension in monthly payments of $833.33.

"One unrealistic assumption will help simplify our illustration. Instead of monthly payments, we'll pretend that the $10,000 per year is payable in one sum, once a year, at the end of each year. The present value of this mythical arrangement can later be adjusted to recognize that payments are really made on a monthly basis.

"We now have a 65-year-old male who will receive $10,000 at age 66, $10,000 at age 67, $10,000 at age 68, and so on. Each payment, of course, is contingent upon our pensioner surviving to that age.

"The first $10,000 payment is due in one year (if our man is alive then), at age 66. The present value of that one payment is something less than $10,000 for two reasons. The first is that money available today will grow with interest during the year, so we need less than $10,000 now in order to have $10,000 in one year.

"A 'judgment call' is required to determine what rate of interest should be used in discounting the $10,000. If we agree to use six percent, standard discount tables will tell us that $9,434 will grow to $10,000 in one year at that rate, so our $10,000 is now reduced to $9,434.

"But the $10,000 is paid only if he survives to age 66. The $9,434 figure would be $10,000 too much should he die before age 66. Such a death has a low probability, but it is a known probability. Using the 1971 Group Annuity Mortality (GAM) Table, which is an appropriate table for pensioners, we find that the probability of a 65-year-old male surviving to age 66 is 97.87 percent.

"We do not know whether this one person will survive the next year, but we do know that the probability of his survival is 97.87 percent, and this knowledge is sufficient to determine present values. We next take 97.87 percent of the $9,434 to arrive at $9,233, which represents the present value of the $10,000 due at age 66. This value is a result of the amount of payment ($10,000), times the one-year six percent discount factor (0.9434), times the probability that the payment will be made (97.87 percent).

"Next we determine the present value of the second $10,000 payment, the potential payment at age 67. We first multiply this by the two-year discount factor, which is six percent per year, compounded. This factor, 0.8900, multiplied by $10,000 equals $8,900.

"From the same GAM mortality table, we find that the probability of a 65-year-old male surviving two years to age 67 is 95.56 percent. We take 95.56 percent of $8,900, which is $8,505, to arrive at the present value of the second $10,000 payment. Again, the formula for this second present value is the amount of payment ($10,000), times the two-year discount factor (0.8900), times the probability that the payment will be made (95.56 percent).

"The procedure for determining the present value of the third $10,000 payment should now be apparent. The value is $10,000 (the amount), times 0.8386 (the three-year discount factor), times 93.05 percent (the probability of survival to age 68) which equals $7,812.

"The individual present values are similarly determined for all potential $10,000 payments. For example, the present value of the tenth payment is $10,000 times 0.5584 times 69.88 percent, which is $3,902. The present values for individual payments keep diminishing as each payment is projected further into the future. For example, the present value is $11 for the potential $10,000 payment at age 100.

"Once we have determined the present value for each year's payment, we know the present value of the entire pension. It is the sum of the individual values, or $9,233 + $8,900 + $7,812 + . . . + $3,902 + . . . + $11 . . ., which equals $87,267.

"The $87,267 value follows from the unrealistic assumption of the pension being paid in annual $10,000 end-of-the-year payments. Changing to monthly payments of $833.33, and using methods not explained here, we arrive at a $92,683 present value.

"Let's review the meaning of this $92,683. It's the actuarial present value for an $833.33 monthly pension payable to a male, age 65, based on the 1971 Group Annuity Mortality Table with interest at six percent a year. Changing the amount of monthly pension, or the pensioner's age or sex, or the assumed mortality table, or the assumed interest rate will change the actuarial present value.

"Note that the $92,683 present value does not imply any specific length of life or use the "life expectancy" of the pensioner. Using the life expectancy to determine a present value is a popular and plausible method, but it is not a correct procedure. It assumes a specific length of life, rather than using a weighted average of values arising from all possible lifetimes."

Note, however, that no attempt has been made in this example to take into account the effect of inflation on the value of the pension payment to the pensioner.

14. The time element can be focused on two parameters: the first, actuarial assumptions and calculations; the second, gift acceptance criteria. Both require data on age, sex, and number of beneficiaries as well as type and terms of agreement.

15. For this study using life insurance industry data as well as Pomona experience, the E&W actuaries selected an appropriate mortality table (see appendix A, E&W Report, sections 3.5.1 and 3.5.2). Comparison with IRS tables will show significant differences since the populations vary substantially.

16. Criteria for the acceptability of gifts subject to a life income or a term for years will more realistically and inexpensively serve the community of charitable institutions than a comprehensive self-analysis of cost-benefit of their planned giving program.

17. Recognizing the fact that all charitable fundraising is more of an art than a science, there should not be a preoccupation with numbers in establishing all development policy, but prudence today suggests that numbers must be a part of the consideration of that policy.

Significantly, most institutions examining costs of their development program have in the past stopped at the acquisition and maintenance cost levels. This was done because budgets provided data that was fixed and computations were largely a matter of arithmetic. That is no longer realistic, and if this study says no more, it is clear that the risk areas where calculated estimates only are possible, cannot be shunted aside. The benefits of a gift program can and should determine the allocation of development resources, the choice of personnel, the marketing strategy, and total gift projections. That in turn, must affect the institutional budgets where gift proceeds are relied upon to balance a budget or acquire new facilities. Everyone involved in a planned gift program must be made aware of the true impact and value of such gifts if they are to act in the best interests of the institution and the donors.

Another way of describing the problem of present value concept is to state that a charity does not receive less value at a future release date on a deferred gift. What it does receive at a future release date is equivalent to a lesser outright gift.

A lesser outright gift which is allowed to compound income and interest over the same period of time as the full term of a deferred gift agreement could have the same value as the remainder when it is released to the institution. In this narrowly defined example, the institution would have to wait the same length of time for either gift (the compounded outright gift or the released remainder) and the value could be the same. All the factors previously described in determining value—particularly the risk factors—would enter into both the rate of discount and the rate of return. What has been illustrated is a comparison of a similar outright gift and a larger deferred gift. The difficulty in making a choice, theoretically, arises from the uncertainties involved in projections.

The Internal Revenue Service, of course, makes its own rules with respect to the value of estate, gift, and income tax charitable deductions. The tables with which the practiced development officer is familiar provide a measure of the charitable deduction for a donor. As many have been saying for a long time, that deductible figure is merely an actuarial calculation and may have little resemblance to the actual value of that remainder. Only experience will prove which number is accurate. The deduction is postulated to be equal to the present value to the charity of the future interest factoring in ages, gender, payout, and type of agreement. Therefore, the determination of the deduction by the Internal Revenue Service equates the value of the outright gift equivalent to the discounted value of the deferred gift as of the date of the transaction.

Implicit in the Internal Revenue Service determination will be actuarial and investment return assumptions. The Internal Revenue Service does not include—nor should it include—factors relating to costs because the differences throughout the

United States among charities will be vast and impossible to codify. In addition to which, such costs are beyond the power or influence of the donor to whom the tax incentive has been granted. A vexatious issue facing the community today in this area is the question of a single sex actuarial table. This reemphasizes the skepticism with which one must approach actuarial issues and answers.

Having outlined those items of cost and calculations which reduce the present value of a gift of a future interest, attention should now be shifted to the benefits of such gifts. The overall conclusion from the Ernst & Whinney Report in the words of that firm are: "The Pomona Plan achieves rates of gift returns which are very attractive in economic terms. It is clear to us that the investment return achieved by the deferred giving programs demonstrates the fundamental economic soundness of these programs."

While the methods used and the specific findings relating to the Pomona Plan are described in detail in the Ernst & Whinney Report and hereinafter in the text of this report, the fact that this kind of computation had not been done before required the application of new theory. The representatives of Ernst & Whinney brought to the discussion expertise in cost accounting, benefit analysis, actuarial projection, and financial management. The authors and William Dunseth represented many years of diversified experience in marketing and managing charitable-giving programs involving outright as well as deferred gifts. Not to be overlooked are the contributions of economists and financial managers. All concurred in the decision to arrive at a common result based on projections using the existing pool of agreements. Benefits were determined on the basis of what is known as the internal rate of return. This concept is normally used by management in determining what is or is not profitable. A rationale for the use of this concept is explained in this report.

The extent of the problem with which we are dealing is perhaps best realized by the need for sound judgment on the part of the trustees or decision makers for any charitable institution. Using the usual board of trustees of a college, for example, the subject of this discussion might well fall within the jurisdiction of several trustee committees including Development, Budget and Finance, Investment, Law, Audit, Real Estate, and even a committee on Plant and Planning.

It is unlikely that one committee will have the expertise to deal with all the questions implicit in a deferred giving program and yet the responsibility for the marketing of a deferred gifts program in an overall development program normally falls with a development committee. The charge to such committees is to raise funds, not necessarily to engage in cost-benefit analyses. Through this study it is suggested that more attention needs be given to these underlying issues prior to the consideration of the marketing of the deferred gifts program. Gift acceptance criteria described in detail later in this report can and should form the rationale of a marketing program. What is to be offered by way of methodical giving and to whom should that effort be directed and on what terms can be determined on the basis of what is best for the institution. In the past the selectivity has been a bootstrap choice of older rather than younger and more rather than less.

Other elements which should be reflected in these determinations are illustrated by the variety of charitable institutions in the United States today. Taking 100 private colleges, for example, there can be 100 different investment programs and 100 different marketing programs. Where the college happens to be located may well determine its ready accessibility to the kind of expertise needed to launch and maintain a successful program. Those institutions which are close to a major city will perhaps benefit more than those that are settled in remote parts of the country. Those institutions with major experience in the management of endowment funds may or may not have an advantage over the emerging institution which has little or no endowment. Many of the factors which are described in this report and set forth in greater detail in the Ernst & Whinney Report should be supplemented according to the experience, difference, and uniqueness of each institution. Guidelines may be useful, but every charitable institution has its own story to tell and as all fundraisers know, it is those exclusive attributes which often make the critical difference in a gift proposal.

The origin of this study is dealt with separately hereinafter. It is not unusual where costs have been investigated before by a charitable institution that outside criteria have been established against which experience and performance were measured. No such preconception has played a part in this study. The facts have been taken as discovered over an extended period of time. The determination to use historical costs to justify projections both as to costs and benefits was made after an examination of other alternatives were researched and tested. The choice was made because it appeared to be the best evidence and would produce a clear and objective result.

The Origin and History of the Pomona Plan

A record of unusual achievement

In 1981 the Pomona Plan was thirty-seven years old and by most standards would be considered a success. Since its beginning, the program has attracted more than $52 million in deferred gifts alone to Pomona College. The total dollar benefit is even larger when one includes bequests and substantial outright gifts contributed by benefactors who first made gifts through annuity and trust plans. As one of the earliest deferred giving programs, the Pomona Plan established a reputation for professional competence and innovation that is evidenced by the more than one hundred requests per year to provide advice and assistance received by the college from other charitable organizations. The inquiries range from the starting of such a program to analytical support on complicated problems from institutions with established deferred giving programs.

The Pomona Plan got its start when Allen Hawley, as Director of Alumni and Public Relations, sought ways in which the college's investment management capabilities could be put to work in the service of friends of the college with little or no personal investment experience. Thinking that the investment of small amounts would hardly be a burden for the college staff and its advisers, Hawley expected that the grateful beneficiaries of this service would leave the invested amount to the college as a bequest. This concept was, of course, later refined as a Life Income agreement and was qualified by the

Internal Revenue Service as a gift of a future interest to a charitable organization.

In reviewing the history of the Pomona Plan, the Pomona College staff members found that enough data was available to provide an overview of the program from its infancy through its adolescence to maturity. However, the data was incomplete and varied considerably in form, making direct comparisons and trend analysis virtually impossible. The data did reveal, however, that much of the Pomona Plan growth had occurred in an especially favorable economic climate. For the first twenty years, there were very low rates of inflation and the potential for capital appreciation of most investments appears in retrospect to have been excellent. During that period, prospective donors from every part of the country wrote to the college expressing an interest in the Pomona Plan, indicating the national appeal of such a program at a time when relatively few institutions offered similar opportunities.

Shortly after those twenty years of gathering financial strength and loyal supporters, the Pomona Plan was tested under new and more difficult conditions. After 1965, national economic conditions changed abruptly. Increased rates of inflation and wide swings in the prices of securities noticeably weakened the confidence of the investment public.

At the beginning of this period of turbulent change, the Revenue Act of 1964 provided for the carry-forward of excess charitable deductions to succeeding tax years, altering the steady and predictable pattern that had characterized deferred giving in earlier decades. In those earlier periods, the typical donor made an annual gift, the size of which was determined by exactly the amount of charitable deduction that could be claimed on that particular year's income tax returns. Consequently, the gifts were relatively small and consisted primarily of cash and securities. The carry-forward provision made it possible for donors to contribute larger gifts, especially using gift assets that had not previously been readily divisible into appropriate increments for smaller gifts, such as real estate parcels.

Inflation continued to swell fair market values by adding apparent value to investments, resulting in more capital gains, whether real or not, to be taxed at still higher tax rates. Charitable remainder plans—which offered the opportunity to avoid capital gains tax entirely, or at least to reduce the tax substantially—represented an important tool for investors. However, the new opportunity to make gifts on a less frequent basis broke the regular rhythm of personal contact each year between Pomona and its donors. Periodic check payments and tax reports did provide communication links, but the personal visit program of college staff calling on donors required new emphasis to keep contacts alive.

The Tax Reform Act of 1969 not only modified the then-current forms of agreements but also made provision for new forms of charitable remainder trusts not previously authorized. Initially, established donors were confused by the changes, and charitable organizations faced a quantum jump in the legal and technical complexities imposed by the new code. No sooner had donors and fundraisers grasped the fundamentals of the new plans than the economy underwent the recession of 1973–1974, during which the values of both stocks and bonds dropped precipitously while interest rates and inflation rates soared. These unfamiliar financial conditions added to the difficulty of managing the new charitable trust agreements. It became evident that none of the benefits under the new forms of agreements were as easily obtained as first thought and that the potential for serious damage to the earning capacity of the trusts was greater than anticipated. The dramatic impact of a new tax law, which was not fully understood for several years after its enactment, coupled with the unusual market conditions filled the period from 1970 to 1975 with uncertainty and misunderstanding for donors and institutions alike.

In the decade of the 1970s donors have contributed to the Pomona Plan at a rate of roughly $2.25 million per year. At the close of the decade, the trend line for the value of new agreements received each year seemed to be rising but additional years of experience will be needed to confirm the trend indication.

The releases to Pomona College from its existing pool of agreements is now projected to be $1 million to $1.3 million a year. While most of the released funds are designated for endowment, the majority of these endowment accounts are available for the general educational purposes of the college.

The average value of bequests and distributions from living trusts (for which Pomona College was not the trustee) during the 1970 decade ranges from $1.5 to $2 million. Roughly, 75 percent of that amount came from non-alumni contributors. While it would not be correct to attribute all non-alumni bequests to Pomona Plan prospects and donors, a substantial portion has resulted from cultivation by deferred giving representatives.

As will be seen, the total value of releases and bequests projected over the next twenty years solely from the agreements in force in July 1, 1978, will vary between $3 million and $5 million a year. These are the funds that for the most part will be available to the college with no additional development effort. Of course, the development costs were paid many years ago to arrive at a point where major additions to the endowment are received virtually free of current development costs. It is the relationship of those long-forgotten costs to the strengthening of the endowment today and tomorrow that is addressed in this study.

Marketing Analysis of the Pomona Plan

A first step.

"Marketing," as the term can be applied to deferred giving programs, has been defined with precision by Linda J. Thoren, an attorney with the firm of Hopkins, Sutter, Mulroy, Davis & Cromartie. Thoren, who has previously served as Director of Deferred Giving at the University of Chicago and as Vice President for Development at the Art Institute of Chicago, said recently at a CASE Conference on Deferred Giving:

> Marketing, then, is the organization's undertaking of *analysis, planning, implementation,* and *control* to achieve its exchange objectives with its target markets.
>
> Exchange is the central concept underlying marketing. It calls for the *offering of value* to someone in exchange for value. Through exchanges various social units, individuals, small groups, and organizations, attain the input they need by giving up something. They acquire something else in return, and normally what they receive is more valued than what they've given up—which explains the motivation for exchange.
>
> A professional marketer is someone who is very good at understanding, planning, and managing exchanges. He knows how to *research* and *understand* the needs of the other party, to design a valued offering to meet these needs, to communicate the offer effectively, and to present it in a good place and under timely circumstances. Marketing is a self-defining term. It means to make an exchange. You have what I want—a service or product—and I have what you want, usually money, we trade, or make a market.

The use of this term "marketing" may offend the antique sentimentalists among development officers who prefer less commercialism in fundraising, but for aggressive programs such as the Pomona Plan, it is entirely appropriate.

With the increasing competition for the philanthropic dollar, a sophisticated application of well-recognized principles is necessary if a charity hopes to attract the maximum support with the resources available, regardless of the category of giving that may be involved. It is essential that individuals who might be prospective donors be identified. Once identified and, when possible, researched, the prospects must be persuaded to include the particular organization and its purposes in their financial plans. The marketer concentrating on deferred gifts must show prospects *how* they can give the maximum within the limitations of their resources and *when* they can give according to their circumstances. All of this falls within the development officer's responsibility to search for new benefactors and cultivate them—not simply to ask for support from obvious and well-established prospects. This is particularly true in the annuity and trust area.

The fundraising program must relate institutional goals to the methods and targets that are selected. Each charitable institution has its own stamp in this process, reflecting its origins, its history, its traditions, and its relationships with contributors. An important common first step in planning is to pinpoint the prospects who will be most interested in deferred giving plans. Tax incentives to charitable giving will play a role with the wealthy because outright gifts substantiate greater tax benefits, but other considerations such as the need or desire to provide a life income to a relative or an employee may encourage the consideration of deferred gifts.

The key target constituency, however, may be those who cannot afford to make a significant outright gift during their lifetime. These are the prospects who can consider an irrevocable gift of relatively large size only if they can retain an income interest for life. To the extent possible, the prospects should be investigated to determine their interests as well as their capacity to give. In any case, likely prospects will place special importance on the retention of income while giving up management control of the assets they donate when the charity or its representative becomes the trustee. It is this irrevocable loss of control which must be emphasized to such donors to insure complete understanding of the nature of life income charitable remainder gifts which qualify for tax deductions.

When the prospective donor has decided to take this important step, primary reasons for this commitment have been, according to Thoren, twofold:

1. The tax benefits, combined with the opportunity to retain needed income, justified a larger gift than would have been possible outright.

2. The plan lets the donor enjoy valuable lifetime tax benefits and psychic rewards by transferring amounts that would otherwise have generated fewer rewards when left as a bequest.

It is with these motivations in mind that Pomona College chose to advertise its deferred giving program to the public by way of newspapers and financial journals. From the inception of the Pomona Plan, the appeal has been made by and large to strangers with no previous tie to the college. Certainly, most of Pomona alumni have become aware of the program through its public recognition, but not as a result of specific advertising targeted at graduates and their parents.

In public advertising, as in individual contacts with prospective donors, it is imperative to be precise and accurate so that nothing is promised that cannot actually be achieved under the tax laws that are then in effect. The tax benefits available through deferred giving agreements are now widely advertised and those benefits are generally available from many qualified charities today. It is the institution itself, its future, and the projects that can be completed with the help of gifts, that will guide the donor in selecting the charitable organization which will benefit from the gift.

Once a prospect has been identified—by alumni volunteers, by advertising, by a referral from a financial adviser—most deferred giving program managers mail promotional literature as part of an educational process. Brochures and letters are used to explain the benefits offered under deferred giving agreements and to highlight the needs of the institution. In addition, the prospect who has more than a passing interest will want to receive factual information about the financial history and the prospects for financial stability in the future of the agency that will manage the prospect's agreement, whether that agency is the business office of the university or a "third party" trustee such as a bank.

Personal contact and communication with prospects is essential to the cultivation process. Thoren has observed that there is commonly a lag time of two to seven years from the time a prospect first considers a deferred gift until the gift is made. The Pomona College marketing analysis, summarized later in this chapter, is generally consistent with a lengthy cultivation period. During that time, the marketer must stay in contact with the prospect. Additionally, personal contact makes it possible to eliminate very quickly those that might be referred to as "non-prospects" (i.e., a person who just wanted the information; the individual who misunderstood the ad in the newspaper; the well-intentioned person who is not financially able to make a deferred gift.)

The first visit is extremely important. The marketer learns as much about the prospect as possible that will shed light on family relationships, financial capability, personal objectives, estate plans, investment interests, and business experience. The marketer should be aware that the prospect is in turn evaluating the trustworthiness and competence of the institution's representative—and from that, the credibility of the institution. The marketer must answer technical questions clearly and accurately—or must be quick to admit that the question must be referred to the program's legal or investment advisers. A knowledgeable and enthusiastic discussion of the institution will enhance its reputation in the prospect's mind and will quite often reveal the specific interests the prospect may have.

Patience is the key to marketing an annuity and charitable trust program. Most prospective donors to Pomona are individuals who cannot afford to give away their savings irrevocably without retaining an income interest. That type of person must know exactly what deferred giving plans can and cannot do. The prospect quite often must weigh the advantages and disadvantages of several plans to choose the one most suitable in terms of satisfying personal objectives. This all takes time. In the case of institutions which, like Pomona, appeal to strangers, there will be time spent in learning more about the institution itself. Additional time will be spent by the prospect in discussing the deferred gift with personal advisers—quite often both legal and tax consultants—before making a definite commitment. Only experience can tell the marketer when to push for a decision. It is clearly better to wait and be helpful than to lose the gift entirely through impatience.

The use of volunteers to market deferred giving agreements requires careful thought. Alumni can be very useful in identifying prospects and in giving a first-hand account of the excellence of the institution. On the other hand, it may be counterproductive to have volunteers who are not thoroughly schooled in the intricacies of annuity and trust tax laws discussing the subject with prospects. At Pomona College, full-time staff representatives are the sole contacts with prospects who are considering deferred gifts.

Pomona Plan Marketing Analysis

In conjunction with the Ernst & Whinney Cost–Benefit Analysis, discussed in chapter 6, the Pomona College staff did a marketing analysis to make it possible to relate the cost effectiveness results with a particular marketing strategy. The marketing analysis sought to define the strategy in terms of prospect identification, prospect cultivation, and a new donor profile. Marketing data was collected for the period 1974–1979—the same five-year period used in evaluating historical costs for the Cost–Benefit Analysis.

In this regard, it should be noted that marketing cost data for the Pomona Staff analysis varies from the Cultivation and Solicitation costs employed in the Ernst & Whinney Report. The cost data within the marketing analysis is internally consistent and supports the conclusions of that study. The data was not intended to be an input into the Cost-Benefit Analysis, which depends on cost information and cost allocation obtained by using a different set of rules.

Prospect identification by advertising in newspapers and magazines has been a technique used by Pomona College for the past thirty-seven years. During the 1974–1979 period, the advertising campaign plan was consistent with the many years of experience prior to 1974. There were adjustments made to meet rising costs for advertising space and to shift to new media when there were signs of declining reader interest. The advertising plan can be characterized by these three factors: the average cost (not indexed for inflation) of obtaining one prospect name from all media has remained constant at about $75 for the five-year period; an increasingly large number of prospects reside outside of the West Coast area, making personal visits by staff members more costly; subjective judgments of field representatives indicate that the overall quality of prospects seems to have improved over the period of the analysis.

During the cultivation phase, Pomona College places greater emphasis on field visits to make personal contact than on mailing promotional literature and solicitation letters. The data for the five-year period showed that about 50 percent of the advertising respondents on the active cultivation list at any given time had been visited at least once. In this case, a visit was defined as an attempt by a college representative to make personal contact by arriving at the mailing address the prospect provided—even if personal contact was not possible. A certain number of advertising respondents will not be visited unless they specifically request a visit. These are respondents who use a post office box as a mailing address, or those who move and leave no forwarding address, or those who live in relatively remote locations that would be expensive in time and money to visit.

The length of time that an advertising respondent should be retained on the active cultivation list is not easily fixed. The marketing analysis revealed that five years after responding to an advertisement, half of the respondents had been dropped from active cultivation and half had been retained. With an on-going advertising program, however, there was little justification to retain a prospect's name on the cultivation list longer than five years if no personal contact had been made or if there was no evidence of interest on the prospect's part.

In estimating the success ratio in converting prospects to donors, the staff compared the number of first-time donors to the average number of prospects on the mailing list during the year. This ratio is a rough approximation only since no attempt was made to account for the turnover (both drops and new additions) of names on the prospect list during any twelve-month period. During this five-year period, about 0.5 percent of the prospects under active cultivation in any given year became new donors. The staff effort devoted to field contacts with prospects amounted to about 2.5 man-years per year for the five years. If the operating cultivation costs (salaries excluded) are allocated among the prospects who were considered to be both accessible and eligible, the cost was about $13 a year per prospect to attract new donors to the program.

Thoren was quoted earlier in this chapter with respect to lag time between a donor's first thought of a deferred gift and the actual gift. The marketing analysis measured the cultivation period from first contact with Pomona College to first agreement. Though the population is admittedly quite small for drawing statistical inferences, two rather distinct groups of donors could be identified. About 35 percent of the new donors during the five years had been cultivated for three years or longer before making a gift. About one-half of the new donors made their first gift in twelve months or less, very possibly indicating a need to solve a specific financial problem within a particular tax year.

It is interesting to note that the percentage representing this second group does not change when new donors who had close ties with the college (alumni, faculty, trustees) are added. That is, if only strangers are included in the analysis, about one-half of the strangers make their first gift in the first year. If those with close ties to the college are added, about one-half of the larger total still falls within the one-year bracket. What is more, all of the donors who had affiliations with the college made the first agreement within one year of the time that first contact was made with the Annuity and Trust Program Office.

It would seem that these loyal supporters of the college were already convinced of the worth of the institution, knew of the program in advance of first contact, and timed their decision to fit their own personal financial planning. The lack of decision making by strangers during the period from twelve months to thirty-six months was striking, however.

A profile of the new donor who most often is also the beneficiary based on the experience over the five years that were studied follows:

The donor (or donors) is/are at least 60 years of age. There is no apparent statistical difference as to the number of male donors, female donors, or married couples as joint donors. It is most likely that the donor resides in Southern California and has no previous affiliation with Pomona College. The cultivation period before the first gift "averages" about two years (although, as pointed out earlier, most of the individual cultivation periods were either less than 12 months or longer than 36 months).

There is no question that marketing the program to donors who have already made at least one deferred gift to Pomona is a very significant factor in assessing the program. "Repeat" gifts from donors account for 75 percent of the new agreements each year—these are the "satisfied customers." The repeat donor's opinion of the college may well be influenced far more by the performance of the college business office and its investment advisers than by the skill of development officers. This is not to suggest that the marketer no longer has a key role. The development field representative must endeavor to assure that the donor's expectations, both as donor and as beneficiary, are being met and that complaints are dealt with promptly, courteously, and personally. At Pomona, donors are visited regularly, usually with greater frequency than prospects. The purposes of these visits are:

1. to learn if the donor is satisfied with the administration of the donor's agreements;

2. to express thanks personally for the donor's support and generosity;

3. to bring the donor up to date on changes in tax laws and college policies;

4. to be available to provide advice for additional agreements or for bequests; and

5. to seek referral of other prospects.

The fact that cultivation objectives are mixed with trust administration functions, for both the development office and the business office, makes detailed cost accounting somewhat difficult. The Ernst & Whinney Cost–Benefit Analysis was based on an arbitrary but reasonable assumption that all costs related to a donor after the *first* agreement had been made would be considered to be agreement maintenance costs.

In summary, Pomona College spent from its operating funds (salaries are not included) about $75 per prospect to acquire the name and an additional $40 to cover the operating costs of cultivation for three years. About 20 percent of the advertising respondents each year were of such potential that they were worth retaining for active cultivation for five years. Unless some specific interest was indicated by a prospect within five years, the prospect was in most cases dropped. Of the prospects under active cultivation at any given time, only a handful could be expected to make a "first" deferred gift in any given year.

Personal contact is essential. All prospects who are reasonably accessible are slated to be visited at least once a year— experience indicates that about 50 percent of the total respondents actually were visited. The best measure of the effectiveness of the deferred giving staff is the number of personal contacts made in a year.

Donors who have already made at least one annuity or trust agreement are clearly the best prospects. "Repeat" gifts represent the largest portion of the new agreements made each year.

Donor attitudes toward the business office function will most strongly influence the likelihood that a donor will make a "repeat" gift. Success lies in the person-to-person persuasion of a donor to choose from a variety of opportunities by which he or she can preserve or increase existing income, make a substantial contribution to future generations of students, and at the same time enjoy the benefit of multiple tax incentives provided by Congress and most state legislatures.

FIVE ▬▬▬▬▬▬▬▬▬▬▬▬▬▬▬▬

What Prompted the Pomona Cost–Benefit Analysis

What's it really worth?

Given the apparent success of the Pomona Plan and its distinctive marketing strategy, why should Pomona College's trustees and senior administrators have wanted to undertake a detailed study of this long-established deferred giving program? Were operating costs growing at an unreasonable rate? Apparently not. When the cost–benefit study was initiated, the deferred giving staff was about the same size that it had been fifteen years before. Operating costs increased at or below the annual rates of inflation. Was there a concern that increasing competition required a more cost-effective program? The Pomona College staff has concerned itself with preparing proposals that would be fair in balancing the interests of the prospective donor with the future interests of the college. It was in the interest of determining what was fair to both parties that the need for a more complete understanding of the cost–benefit relationship was recognized—not to engage in some form of bidding competition for a donor's support.

Demands for cost-effectiveness data for the Annuity and Trust Program had come from several sources, and some had been under discussion for years. The matter of determining a more accurate means of valuing the charitable remainder interest took on new importance in the light of two new developments affecting the future of Pomona College. The first event was the planning for the college's centennial year in

1987. The plan to reaffirm the academic excellence of the college in the coming decade called for a careful reconsideration of development objectives. It was clear that the Annuity and Trust Program, as successful as it may have been, had not produced sufficient endowment funds to offset the erosive effects of inflation—much less to meet the changing needs of the college.

In *The History of Pomona College* (1977), E. Wilson Lyon, President Emeritus of Pomona, traced in great detail the means that were used to meet the financial crises that occurred in the first eighty years of the college's life. He recounted that in 1962, the seventy-fifth anniversary year, a capital gifts campaign was undertaken. In Lyon's words: "Some trustees felt that the very successful life-income contract program would meet the college's need. But this income lay in the future and could not supply the pressing current demands" (p. 512).

Significantly, Lyon's term of office, the longest in the history of the college, spanned the first twenty-five years of growth of the Pomona Plan. Incidentally, during the 1962 campaign, the annuity and life-income gifts of more than $2 million per year were not even counted as part of the capital campaign. The search for the proper balance between outright giving and deferred giving in today's development effort is as complicated now as it was earlier, not only by the delay in receiving the benefits, but also by the fact that once having entered into deferred gift contracts inescapable costs arise from the college's legal commitments to administer the agreements until they are terminated.

The second event occurred when, on relatively short notice, college officials decided that a major reorganization of the Pomona business office was to be completed by July 1979. The Annuity and Trust Management section of the business office had been responsible for administration of gift annuities, pooled fund agreements, and charitable remainder trusts. This section was responsible for important technical functions such as accounting records, tax reports, check payments, custodianship of legal documents and assets, releasing the trust remainders to the college, and many other related activities. In anticipation of a complete turnover of personnel and major changes in business office operating procedures, staff planners realized that better decisions involving staffing and functional matters could be made if they were based on a cost–benefit analysis that included the impact of business office perform- ance on donor relations and other marketing activities.

Cost-effectiveness data had been needed for some time in the management of the Pomona Plan. In 1972, William Dun- seth, then Director of the Annuity & Trust Program and later to become Vice President for Development at Pomona, rec- ognized the need to prepare written guidelines and policies, which were in turn approved by the Pomona College Board of Trustees. Those guidelines, based on good judgment and many years of operating experience, served Pomona well and were widely circulated to other charitable institutions at their request. However, the guidelines were developed without the benefit of cost-revenue analysis. It was recognized that such an analysis might well show the need for new standards of evaluating proposed agreements as well as for modifying in- vestment objectives for separately managed trusts.

In the past, Pomona College management reports had simply incorporated goals and accomplishments in terms of the fair market value of deferred gifts under the Pomona Plan—that is, the amount the donor transferred to the college. Most often the reports included no reference to program cost beyond a comment as to whether or not the operating budget of the Annuity and Trust Department had been exceeded. When cost–benefit evaluations were made, they were quick and easy attempts to measure the effectiveness of the Development Off- ice alone rather than all of the organizations and activities involved in the deferred giving program. These somewhat oversimplified approaches were constant reminders that better management reporting procedures were needed.

The members of the Pomona College Board of Trustees like- wise have needed accurate cost-effectiveness data to oversee the Pomona Plan. The Investment Committee of the Board of Trustees traditionally reviewed and approved each annuity and trust agreement. While the review of each agreement for conformance to approved policy has been thoughtful, the trustees were not able to take the time to review in detail the full scope of the program, to include marketing. The trustees, it was determined, could function with even greater effectiveness if they had the benefit of program management reports, which emphasized forecasting future financial benefits, indexing techniques to account for inflation, cost trends, and investment alternatives. The cost-effectiveness study was well suited to assemble the information and develop a format for reporting on a continuing basis. The study results were expected to suggest that the current policy and guideline statement be revised and approved by the trustees, giving them the opportunity to set the direction for future program activities and to revise management standards for new agreements.

In preparing to satisfy the internal demands for cost-effectiveness data, Pomona College recognized that the study results would also be useful for the many institutions that were considering the establishment of their own deferred giving programs. A Study steering committee—composed of trustees, faculty members, staff administrators, and top development officials at other universities who had experience with deferred giving programs—undertook to define the study approach and objectives in the light of these multiple requirements.

Having reviewed the historical record of the Pomona Plan, the steering committee members directed special attention to one of the unique features of the program: advertising in newspapers and magazines appealing for public support through the Pomona Plan. The thought to turn to advertising at the very outset followed the decision by the Board of Trustees not to offer the Pomona Plan to alumni and parents, in order to protect the annual giving program. Since then, other colleges and universities have joined in advertising their deferred giving programs in public media although there is a large segment of the higher education community that is uncomfortable with public advertising.

The potential to attract strangers to support the college led the steering committee to think in terms of a Pomona Plan analysis that might serve as a decision-making model for the many private colleges and universities throughout the nation with small alumni bodies and a need to build up an endowment fund. Furthermore, a decision to undertake a deferred giving program at this time in the hope of rescuing or at least of strengthening the future financial posture of an institution could be made with more confidence if based on a dependable estimate of the initial costs during the period when little or no revenue would flow to the institution. Decision makers would also require a reasonable prediction of the probable dates of release as well as the true value of benefits when made available to the institution.

The committee members agreed that to be most useful in providing a model, the cost-effectiveness study of the Pomona Plan would require some corroborating data from other educational institutions to indicate that the evaluation method was practical and that Pomona's experience could be considered typical. The study would also have to evaluate the chances for success of a new program initiated in today's economic and social environment rather than the 1940–1960 period during which the Pomona Plan became firmly established. The committee members came to see the proposed study effort not as a narrow case of self-examination but rather as an opportunity to offer a helping hand to financially troubled colleges throughout the nation at a crucial time.

In 1977, an additional need for cost–benefit information arose in an unforeseen way. In response to highly publicized incidents that raised questions as to the fundraising practices of certain charitable organizations, Congress took under consideration legislative proposals that would require public disclosure of charitable fundraising costs. In September 1977, Senator Mark Hatfield of Oregon wrote to the American Association of Fund Raising Counsel, acknowledging the complexity of the issues involved and stating his desire to avoid additional federal intrusion into philanthropic and religious activities:

> The issue of disclosure of charitable fund raising costs has turned out to be much more complicated than I first appreciated. Although many are anxious to have legislation enacted in Congress that will reduce the possibility of fraudulent activity and excessively expensive administration among nonprofit organizations, it is important that sufficient time be given to study the ramifications of a draft such as the one I have been preparing. Further, I want to await the results of

the efforts of the charitable organizations to establish their own policies of voluntary self-disclosure. Some people whom I respect have suggested that it is possible for this to be done rather than to have additional federal intervention into the philanthropic and religious communities.

The problem area being addressed by federal legislators has been complicated by related actions of an increasing number of state legislatures. John J. Schwartz, President of the American Association of Fund Raising Counsel, pointed out in 1978 that twenty-one states already had percentage limitations on the costs of fundraising, and thirty-five states had legislation regulating fundraising activities. The resulting requirements for registration of charities, detailed reporting of fiscal and management information, and prescribed disclosure of fundraising costs have created difficult administrative problems for charitable organizations. The prospect of more states adopting similar laws will add to the problem.

With increasing legislative interest in public disclosure of fundraising costs, it became important to report deferred giving costs in an accurate and understandable form. Even if the reports to the public were accurate, there was the possibility that donors might conclude that organizations with the lowest fundraising costs were the most deserving of support.

There are, of course, a number of valid reasons for fundraising costs to differ among charities—reasons that are in most cases unrelated to efficiency. It would not be easy to arrive at a fair method of reporting cost data that would not be misunderstood by the public. Of all types of fundraising the deferred giving program presents unique difficulties in relating costs and revenues. As state legislatures attempt to arrive at measures to protect donors from a few irresponsible organizations, the diversity of the resulting statutes may add significantly to the costs of fundraising programs and could place serious geographical and procedural limitations on a large number of otherwise efficient programs.

The ability to make meaningful comparisons among several fundraising programs is fundamental both to internal decision making affecting staffing and budget allocations and to the accuracy of public disclosure statements. Stephen J. Smallwood and Wilson C. Levis, in an article titled "The Realities of Fund-Raising Costs and Accountability," have discussed methods of providing fair and understandable fundraising costs in a public statement. They argued that legitimate costs can be expected to vary considerably among different charitable organizations and among distinctive fundraising categories, such as new donor acquisition, donor renewal, and capital programs. Further, they concluded that the use of a single ratio measurement for an active development program could be very misleading. In commenting on the deferred gifts and bequest category as an element of a total fundraising program, Smallwood and Levis also recognized the complexities involved:

> Worse, the summary revenue–cost ratio approach is further skewed beyond acceptability where a deferred giving program and/or a charitable bequest program is concerned. This is because there is no correlation between the costs expended in a particular year for either or both of these programs and the support provided by the programs. An institution may expend funds during a year to establish and disseminate information about its pooled income fund and/or charitable remainder trust programs and not experience any return from the program(s) until several years later. Likewise, an organization may devote dollars to the formation of a bequest program and succeed in causing individuals to make provision for it in their wills and not receive any money in return for years to come. In either instance, the funds flow to the charity as the result of happenstance (usually at individual's death); the fund-raising costs associated with such programs cannot realistically be related to the receipts generated by the programs. (p. 10)

The same problem of relating current costs with future receipts is faced in allocating resources among the various segments of a fundraising activity. This problem would be minimized if fundraisers were less specialized and could negotiate deferred agreements with major donors as part of a larger contribution package. Again, less rigid organizational and budget categories are needed if fundraising efficiency is to be improved and if the multipurpose requirements of major donors are to be met.

As noted earlier, the adequacy of the cost–benefit relationship of deferred gifts was questioned in a 1973 *Harvard Business Review* article by Vincent A. Fulmer. The principal subject of his article was the need to discount long-term pledges in the light of prevailing interest rates. In passing, Fulmer took note of the life-income agreement in terms of true worth and acquisition cost:

> Discounted value weighs heavily in calculating the worth of certain types of gifts where the pay-in period is very long or where the donor retains a life interest in the income from his gift—as in the case of a charitable-remainder trust. The principal value of this kind of fund raising is not the immediate net dollar gain to the institution but the construction of a framework of enlightened self-interest in which to engage prospective donors through often delicate discussion of their estate plans.
>
> Charitable-remainder trusts are an increasingly important means of encouraging persons to make valuable and meaningful long-term gifts to institutional endowments. But they can also be expensive gifts to raise, in terms of foregone lifetime giving and in terms of expense in securing and servicing them. (p. 107)

The question of exchanging outright unrestricted gifts for deferred agreements (the remainders from which might well be restricted by the donor) concerned Fulmer as it had the Pomona College trustees in 1944. In part, Pomona College has not had to face this issue since most of the Pomona Plan donors have had no ties to the college and would probably not have made any gift to the college were it not for the specific benefits offered under the Pomona Plan. But the issue of discounting the value of deferred gifts and relating the discounted value to the program costs could not be sidestepped.

In reviewing techniques that were available for making a cost–benefit analysis, the Pomona College staff concluded that none of the existing analytical methods was completely satisfactory. The methods had been developed in the early 1970s, in some instances at Pomona College and in other cases at other colleges with deferred giving programs. It was decided by the steering committee that a computational model that would satisfy the stated needs might be quite intricate and could best be formulated by professionals who had experience with present value calculations and cost-indexing computations. Pomona College then contracted with Ernst & Whinney (then Ernst & Ernst) to direct the data retrieval effort and to make the cost–benefit analysis. In establishing the objectives for this analytical study, considerable stress was placed on the development of a general method that could be used by any institution to evaluate or estimate the cost–benefit ratio of a deferred giving program. The study objectives and major questions to be answered were approved by the steering committee:

I. Historical Analysis (1944–1978)

A. Collect data for each Pomona College annuity and trust agreement; including:

1. Type of plan: intervivos or testamentary; organization or individual serving as trustee.

2. Initial asset value; value at time of release or current market value for agreements still in force; stated investment objectives and implementing investment strategies.

3. Assets by type: appreciated or unappreciated.

4. Date agreement established and ages of beneficiaries at that time; date of release of agreement remainder to college; for agreements in force, number of beneficiaries still living and their ages.

B. Collect information concerning donors to the Pomona Plan:

1. Source and date of first contact, relationship (alumni, strangers, and so on); follow-on contacts (in person, by mail, and so on); state of residence.

2. Number of Pomona Plan agreements for each donor; asset value for each agreement.

3. For donors who came in contact with the college through the Pomona Plan, amount of subsequent outright gifts and/or bequests.

C. For the Pomona Plan, collect full cost information:

1. Cost of acquiring agreements (advertising, travel expenses, appraisal fees, and so on).

2. Cost of managing agreements (business office, legal counsel, investment counsel, and so on).

D. To the extent possible, evaluate the staffing patterns and operating efficiency as related to overall effectiveness and cost factors; the adequacy of professional fees compared with typical fees charged for similar services.

    E. Develop methods and models to:

        1. Allocate costs to the Pomona Plan and to individual agreements.

        2. Index to a base year the following: costs, payments to beneficiaries, initial value, release values.

II. Comparative Data for Other Selected Colleges and Universities

    A. Annuity and trust agreements in force; total of releases to date.

    B. Asset values: initial, current, or at release.

    C. Policies governing acceptance of new agreements; investment guidelines.

    D. In-house or third-party trustee.

    E. Staffing and operating costs for deferred giving program.

III. Cost–Benefit Analysis

    A. Full cost per dollar of new contracts; full cost per dollar of release value.

    B. Define a standard chart of accounts.

    C. Ratio of release values to initial values.

    D. Ratio of initial values to related costs of acquiring agreements.

    E. Relate effects of legislation/revenue rulings to cost–benefit ratio changes.

    F. Define the degree to which Pomona Plan values deviate from norms reported by other colleges and universities in the study sample.

    G. Describe model for annual cost–benefit management reports.

    H. Develop models to project:

        1. Release dates.

        2. Release values in current dollars, base-year dollars, and future dollars (forecast GNP deflator).

        3. Full costs.

As noted earlier in this report, it was only after Pomona

College financial records had been examined by the Ernst & Whinney team that it became apparent that the analysis of historical data as outlined above was not practical. At that point, the study directors agreed with the senior representative from Ernst & Whinney that an analysis based on projecting the program's internal rate of return was the most realistic approach to satisfying the study objectives.

SIX ███████████████████████

Summary of the Pomona
Cost–Benefit Analysis

The bottom line and how to get there.

Pomona College under the terms of the grant received from the Lilly Endowment contracted with Ernst & Whinney to develop a methodology to evaluate the cost–benefit ratios of deferred giving programs and specifically to evaluate the cost effectiveness of the Pomona Plan. Expressed another way, is the return achieved by the Pomona deferred giving program sufficient to justify the expenditures incurred to realize that return? The final report from Ernst & Whinney annexed as appendix A speaks for itself. The summary which follows highlights those portions of the study that are of special importance and comments on some of the theoretical treatments in the document.

Recognizing that no two charitable institutions are likely to have deferred giving programs with the same organization and structure from gift promotion to final distribution, the conclusions as to cost per dollar for Pomona, while important to Pomona, are less important to the interested reader than the methods by which those conclusions were reached. Some of the Pomona Plan results are interesting, however, because they define the ways in which program effectiveness can be evaluated:

1. The acquisition cost per dollar for 1,808 agreements in force as of June 30, 1978, aggregating $35,632,000, was 8.7¢ (see appendix A, E&W Report, section 4.5 and table 5.2.3).

2. The acquisition cost per dollar for outright bequests over the base period was 2.2¢ (E&W, section 4.1, step 12; section 4.5; and table 5.3.3).

3. Based on the "Wharton Expected Case," the cost per dollar translates as follows:

    a) For the 213 gift annuities, 66¢ per dollar, or an internal rate of return of 51.9%;

    b) For the 1,190 gifts of pooled income funds, 78¢ per dollar, or an internal rate óf return of 27.7%;

    c) For the 405 separately managed unitrusts and annuity trusts, 84¢ per dollar or an internal rate of return of 18.4% (E&W, sections 3.7, 4.5, and tables 4.5.1, 5.1.7).

4. Based on the "Wharton Expected Case," the internal rate of return on all deferred gifts including outright bequests attributable to the Pomona Plan was 92%. The addition of bequests with its very low direct costs at 2.2¢ per dollar measurably enhanced the rate of return.

5. Over twenty years it is possible to project the following releases of principal to Pomona College. a) annuities—84%; b) pooled income funds—56%; c) separately managed trusts—52% (E&W, sections 3.6.6 and 4.3).

6. Based upon 1,500 lives (E&W, section 3.5.1) of which 43.5% were male and 56.5% were female, the combined aggregate one-life table compared favorably to the Society of Actuaries 1971 individual annuity mortality table adjusted by a 10% decrease in mortality. (E&W, section 3.5.2; section 4.1, step 7; section 4.3).

7. Agreement maintenance costs (see E&W, table 5.1.3), while less in aggregate than acquisition costs in each year of the study, had to be projected over the life of the agreements. Separately managed trusts imposed the heaviest cost burden at 85% of the annual maintenance expenses, with pooled funds at 10% and annuities at 5%. (E&W, table 5.1.5).

The yearly allocation of such costs, i.e. trust administration fees, custodial fees and real property expenses are set forth in table 5.1.6 of the E&W Report. An approximate average for the annual maintenance cost ratio was derived by the authors using values from E&W Report, table 5.1.6 (cost by gift category) and table 5.2.3 (dollar value under management by gift category). An average of maintenance expenditures for the five-year period was divided by the amount under management on June 30, 1978, to arrive at costs per dollar:

a) Gift annuities: 0.2¢ per dollar under management.

b) Pooled income fund: 0.2¢ per dollar under management.

c) Separately managed trusts: 1¢ per dollar under management.

d) Total for all gift categories: 0.5¢ per dollar under management.

As is the case with many research projects, there is an evolutionary pattern that the Ernst & Whinney analysts and the study directors followed as initial efforts appeared to lead the study down a deadend road—or, at least, a road that was seriously constricted by very narrow bridges. To avoid these obstacles, the most notable change at the outset was the decision to project values and costs into the future rather than to attempt a retrospective analysis of the actual history of the Pomona Plan.

Originally, it was anticipated that the Ernst & Whinney study would assemble historical data—the amount of money already released to the college over the previous thirty-five years and the amount of costs incurred in obtaining those benefits. That historical analysis was expected to adjust all values (costs and benefits) for inflation and then to examine the relationship between actual costs and benefits. This approach to Pomona's experience was dropped when it became apparent that the earlier accounting records of the college were not sufficiently detailed to support this type of cost analysis and that the management changes imposed by the Tax Reform Act of 1969 were so dramatic that data for the period before 1969 was of doubtful value. In effect, the analysts were forced to project future program costs and future benefit values (see appendix A, E&W Report, section 3.2.1).

The analysts developed procedures to predict the value of the amounts that would probably be released from agreements for use by the college during the period 1978–1998 (E&W, tables 5.3.1 and 5.3.2) and to project the cost of managing those agreements for that twenty-year period (E&W, table 4.5.2).

The reliability of those projections depends on: 1) the ability to predict mortality experience accurately; 2) the precision with which the econometric models (such as those formulated by the Wharton School of the University of Pennsylvania, UCLA, and others) can be used to estimate inflation rates and investment yields; and 3) the validity of projecting costs twenty years into the future by extrapolating from average costs incurred over the past five years.

From a layman's point of view, the section of the Ernst & Whinney Report devoted to projection of expected mortality rates (E&W, section 3.5) is an understandable description of the steps taken to represent the population of Pomona donors and payees by a mortality table, which in turn is related to insurance industry tables. Lest the reader conclude that this mortality table is anything but an educated guess, the following excerpt from the Transactions of the Society of Actuaries 1979 addresses the issue directly:

> The necessity of using conservative mortality assumptions in pricing annuities is well recognized. The following issues are important in deciding upon a mortality basis. Few companies write a sufficiently large volume of single premium immediate annuity business to develop their own mortality tables. Even on an industry-wide basis, the volume of mortality experience under annuity contracts is far smaller than that under life insurance contracts, adding to the difficulty of establishing credible industry tables.

Accordingly, the Ernst & Whinney table should be viewed as a best estimate made by trained actuaries experienced in making this type of analysis for insurance companies.

In a similar fashion, the growth in the amount of bequests over the period 1980–1998 is simply an extrapolation from a trend line calculated by Ernst & Whinney analysts for the period 1965 through 1979 (E&W, table 5.3.4). It is interesting to note, however, that a three-year average amount for bequests received in the period 1979–1981, inclusive, is extremely close to the Ernst & Whinney projected receipts for the same period. Nevertheless, it must be recognized that the twenty-year projection is not based on "expectancies"—known or suspected; nor on program plans to solicit bequests; nor on an analysis of the full potential of a college bequest program. The sustained growth shown in table 5.3.4 of the Ernst & Whinney Report (see appendix A) is a statistical insight based on an assumption that the growth rate in the past will continue unabated with no known limit to the total receipts that can be anticipated. This statement is not intended to be critical of the analysis as much as to draw attention to the nature of the uncertainties that are unavoidable when twenty-year projections must be made.

The results of the Ernst & Whinney analysis of the Pomona Plan are summarized in an *internal annual rate of* return computed for each type of agreement (i.e., gift annuities, pooled income funds, and charitable remainder trusts). The following extended definition of the term *internal rate of return* is quoted from the Ernst & Whinney Report:

> The calculation method applied is the internal rate of return (IRR), which is defined as the [annual] interest rate which equates the present value of the expected receipts from agreements in force to the cost of obtaining those receipts.
>
> While the percentage returns which result from the IRR can be expressed in the traditional cost per dollar of gifts received, there are significant differences which should be noted. Most traditional annual and capital giving fundraising programs, as distinct from deferred gift programs, do not require continued management efforts after the gift has been received. The cost per dollar of gift measure is clearly the cost of obtaining the right to receive dollars. It does not address the question of when those dollars will be received—which is the pivotal question in deferred giving. It does not address those situations in which two types of costs are incurred: the cost of obtaining a gift agreement and the cost of managing that agreement during the period of its existence. *Therefore, the traditional measurement of costs per dollar of gift received does not address the economic complexities of deferred fundraising programs.* (Emphasis added)

The internal annual rates of return, previously described are:

Gift annuities	52%
Pooled funds	28%
Separately managed trusts	18%
Weighted average	28%

The weighted average of 28 percent based on the book value

of agreements in force on June 30, 1978, suggests a precision of results not warranted by the assumptions and approximations inherent in actuarial calculations—much less those inherent in econometric forecasts of inflation indices and market yield factors. We would conclude, therefore, *that 20 percent to 30 percent is a reasonable estimate of the annual internal rate of return for the Pomona Plan without including bequests.*

It is worth noting that a separate rate of return was computed for each form of agreement because it was anticipated that there would be substantial differences in costs associated with the management of one form of agreement as compared to another. Of course, the variation in the number of agreements in each category for one year makes it difficult to make a judgment. The variability of judgments on the allocation of costs is already evident from the three institutional reports included in this study. For example, the Pomona staff estimated that 85 percent of the total maintenance costs each year was expended on separately managed trusts. Wellesley reported only 37 percent of the maintenance effort as being applied to this category. Grinnell initially reported 75 percent as an educated guess of the cost allocations to unitrusts and annuity trusts. These differences may be a function of the volume of agreements under management or perhaps of the nature of the investment management program.

The Ernst & Whinney study views the Pomona Plan as a successful financial venture providing a 20 to 30 percent return on investment. This is analagous to an institution assuming full management of an insurance company to generate profits of 20 percent to 30 percent on investment as a means of obtaining financial support for the college. While this may be a useful measure for determining the true worth of a deferred giving program to an institution when compared to the return that can be realized from other investment opportunities, it is not at all evident that the internal rate of return can be used to make a meaningful comparison with other development programs. Outright giving programs may depend to an extent on cultivation costs spent over a period of years, but there is no need to project benefits—or management costs—over an extended period of time. In fact, the total investment return for an outright gift account is not a factor in valuing the outright gift (although it may be most relevant to the determination of development budget allocations in any given year), whereas investment management is an important factor in calculating the present value of a deferred gift. No doubt a basis for comparing the ultimate net dollar benefit of deferred gifts with outright gifts can be devised, but it is not a function of this study to do so.

The question of comparability aside, however, the inclusion of outright bequests as part of the internal rate of return computations for a deferred giving program which inevitably leads to bequests and testamentary trusts is another matter. Bequest receipts were included in the analysis of the deferred giving program for two reasons: 1) Most educational institutions include the bequest program with the Annuity and Trust Program under a single administrator; 2) It would be difficult to separate out the time and effort which is spent in soliciting a bequest through a discussion of an estate plan while cultivating a prospect from the time devoted to planning a lifetime deferred gift. Frequently, a donor will consciously choose between placing an important asset in trust immediately or retaining control of the asset and making a testamentary disposition.

In some instances, the institution may actually prefer the bequest alternative if management difficulties might be encountered in a trust. In the Ernst & Whinney analysis, only those cultivation costs (2.2¢ per dollar received) expended directly in support of the bequest program (e.g., direct mail, brochures) were charged to bequests. The result is a highly favorable cost–benefit ratio for bequests which, while well deserved, may be somewhat overstated as a consequence of the cost allocation rule.

In considering the general application of these study results, bear in mind that the Pomona Plan may be a "worst case," in the jargon of the economists, because of the marketing strategy employed. Dealing primarily with non-alumni through advertising involves more visits, more persuasion, and perhaps less sentiment. Such donors understandably want to strike the best deal and may be less inclined to adjust their expectations than those who start with a sense of obligation to their alma mater.

What was learned from the Ernst & Whinney analysis can be summarized as follows:

1. The cost of acquiring deferred giving agreements from new donors is relatively inexpensive. At Pomona, the cost was 8.7¢ for each dollar contributed to an agreement; at Wellesley it was half as much (about 4.3¢); Grinnell reported about 2¢.

2. Maintenance costs are somewhat higher than acquisition costs but still are nominal. An overall cost of 1.3¢ per year for each dollar under management appears to be the most that has been paid by the reporting colleges. Nonetheless, over a period of years during which costs are assumed to rise with inflation, the total maintenance costs are shown to be 2.5 times greater than the acquisition costs spent in soliciting the agreements.

3. The major "cost" to the deferred giving program is the amount by which the college's remainder interest is discounted in determining the gift's present value. In effect, the opportunity cost of not having the gift amount available immediately most diminishes its value to the institution.

4. Minimum acceptance criteria which circumscribe the kinds and terms of deferred gift agreements an institution will undertake provide the practical means by which the profitability (i.e., benefits vs. costs) of an agreement can be weighed. The criteria for defining the *duration* of the projected management period is the single factor with the greatest impact on profitability.

5. The investment management of charitable remainder gift agreements must be capable of responding quickly and prudently to the changes in the marketplace. Unlike the management of endowment funds, where a decision can be made each year regarding the expenditure rate and the need to economize, there is no such latitude where specific payments are required under the irrevocable terms of a deferred giving agreement.

6. The rate of return on cost for the Pomona Plan represents a successful fundraising investment. The study has provided the framework for improving the return on investment by being more selective in the agreements that are accepted.

7. The methodology developed for this analysis is complicated and calls for many individual calculations. The computer program

prepared by Ernst & Whinney does not lend itself to use by institutions with small deferred giving programs for which manual calculations would be most practical. The Ernst & Whinney method is an analytical tool most suitable for large, diversified planned giving programs.

The Ernst & Whinney study of the Pomona College program served the two important purposes of establishing a basic analytical methodology for measuring the current value of deferred giving programs and of identifying the factors which have the greatest impact on the program's ultimate benefits.

Testing the Methodologies

What's in it for me?

Once the Ernst & Whinney team completed the analysis of the Pomona College cost–benefit data, the next step was to attempt to document the analytical method. The extensive marketing and management experience which had been accumulated in the administration of the Pomona Plan was the prototype used to design the data retrieval effort and to develop the measures of cost effectiveness. The Ernst & Whinney methods for analyzing the Pomona Program, however, depended heavily on calculations that had to be performed on a computer. Using modern technology, the accounting firm, with the aid and assurances of the co-directors, had achieved one of the initial objectives of the study, namely, the capacity to measure the cost effectiveness of the Pomona Plan.

As described in the preceding chapter, the principal and income accounts for each agreement in force were projected individually, year by year, for twenty years into the future. Each one-year computation took into account cash flow (payment compared to investment return), maintenance costs which varied with inflation rates, effects of inflation on market values, changes in dividend and bond interest rates, and a fractional release of the principal from each agreement, the size of the release being determined by the individual probability that any one agreement might be terminated in a particular year. This calculation utilized a computer program that depended on access to reference tables containing extensive mortality data and econometric projections for each of the twenty years. The numerous computations, interrelated as they were, had been dealt with handily by computer, but it was virtually impossible to describe the calculations in terms that would make manual computations practical for most charitable institution representatives.

The search for a simpler method that would not require computers was then assigned to Ernst & Whinney. The study co-directors suggested that work sheets be designed that would record historical data in a logical and orderly manner and would then prescribe the needed manual computations utilizing the data and reference tables to determine a cost-benefit ratio. This shortcut method would necessarily involve fewer computational steps and hence more approximations than the computer program. The Ernst & Whinney study team concluded that simplification of computational procedures, though possible, could lead to inaccuracies, the extent of which could not be ascertained.

The result of the follow-on effort by Ernst & Whinney is described in section 6 of their report (see appendix A). The shortcut method is contained in fifteen work sheets that provide for the inclusion of gift annuities, pooled income funds, charitable remainder unitrusts and annuity trusts, and outright bequests as separate categories in an internal rate of return calculation. The computations can be done by hand—though a special hand calculator may be used in making the estimate of the internal rate of return.

Standard financial management texts, such as Weston & Brigham's *Managerial Finance*, contain tables which list the present value of a dollar for periods of up to thirty years and for rates of return from 1 percent to 90 percent. These tables make it possible to estimate the internal rate of return if it does not exceed 90 percent.

The shortcut method prepared by Ernst & Whinney includes four reference tables: Projections of Inflation Rates (Wharton Projection, E&W, table 6.2.1); Mortality Release factors based on the investigation of the Pomona Plan (E&W, table 6.2.2); Summary of Investment Rates of Return for various types of deferred giving agreements (Wharton Projection, E&W, table 6.2.3); and Factors for Converting Book Values to Fair Market

Values (Wharton Projection, E&W, table 6.2.4). These tables, it should be noted, reflect Pomona Plan values, which had been gathered from an experience which appeared to be quite different from many other colleges and universities. Specifically, the mix of ages and genders among the income beneficiaries and the proportion of equities to fixed-income securities in the investment portfolios could have a significant effect on the results of the analysis.

Notwithstanding all the uncertainties inherent in projections, both actuarial and econometric, and the unanswered question of the applicability of the Pomona analysis to the general case, other selected educational institutions and one noneducational charity were asked to test the shortcut method with their own experience which in each case differed from Pomona and each other.

The purpose of these tests was to determine if the shortcut method was a practical one, especially for institutions with little or no previous experience with deferred giving, and to ascertain whether or not the analytical results obtained from Pomona's data could be considered typical when compared to other educational institutions having well-established deferred giving programs. With the latter purpose in mind, seven educational institutions and one noneducational charitable organization were invited to participate in the test phase. They were Dartmouth, Wellesley, University of Tennessee, Notre Dame, Grinnell, Stanford, M.I.T., and the Salvation Army. Two institutions, while acknowledging the merit of the objectives, declined the invitation at the outset.

Representatives of the remaining six met with the co-directors and with Ernst & Whinney team leaders to discuss the purposes of the test and to review the detailed use of the methodology. As the participating schools began to retrieve their own data, it became apparent that the effort required to accumulate cost and benefit information from institutional records was going to be extremely time-consuming and expensive. Funds from the Lilly Endowment Grant had been available to pay for student researchers and for Ernst & Whinney field supervisors during the Pomona College data collection phase. No funds were available to support the test organizations, since it had been anticipated that the amount of data to be collected would be substantially less at other schools and that self-interest would motivate each participant to help evaluate its own program.

Unfortunately, without external financial support and professional supervision, all of the test organizations but two were precluded by other institutional priorities from completing the project despite the best of intentions. The data retrieval requirements were more than these institutions, many of which were in the middle of major fundraising campaigns, could undertake on anything but a sporadic basis. Furthermore, the manner in which cost–benefit results were to be computed was complex making it difficult to communicate to other staff who had to perform the detailed work. What had been learned was: A cost–benefit analysis of deferred giving programs is not easily reduced to a shortcut method. This is due to the highly interwoven nature of factors such as contractual terms, income and payout rates, and mortality experience.

Nevertheless, the results submitted by Wellesley and Grinnell showed that the method could be used and the trial computations revealed limiting aspects of the procedures in performing the evaluation of the programs.

From these submissions, it has been possible to evaluate the type of data available, to review the computations performed in accordance with the instructions furnished with the shortcut method, and to compare the results with the Pomona Plan analysis. The responding institutions, despite the pressures of other priorities, did an outstanding job of collecting data completely and with obvious attention to detail. The care taken in recording the data made it possible for the study directors themselves to calculate the cost-benefit ratio when the submitting organization was not able to complete the calculations with the instructions which had been provided. The completed work sheets are included as appendix B.

The three deferred giving programs analyzed offer marked contrasts. Pomona College with some 1,800 agreements, many of which were the simpler pre-1969 forms of Pooled Fund contract, and with $35 million under management, showed substantial amounts in each form of agreement. Grinnell, on the other hand, with 50 agreements valued at more than $5 million had almost 95 percent of the money under management in separately managed trusts. Wellesley had about $3.5 million in about 175 deferred giving agreements, with benefits almost equally divided among gift annuities, pooled fund, and unitrusts (there were no annuity trusts reported). Thus, the number of agreements under management differed as did the predominant types of agreement.

The constituencies supporting each college's deferred giving program were quite different as well. As noted earlier, Pomona College made its appeal primarily to individuals with no prior connection with the college. Support for Wellesley came from its alumnae, with some evidence that gift annuities may have been used to establish class endowment programs. A significant number of Grinnell's agreements came from its trustees and most of the remaining agreements came from alumni. In calculating Grinnell's overall rate of return (appendix B work sheet), bequest benefits were included in arriving at a rate in the range of 100 percent to 150 percent. The Wellesley rate of return, without including bequest projections, was calculated to be 50 percent to 60 percent (appendix B work sheet). The Pomona rates of return were found to be 20 percent to 30 percent without considering bequests and above 90 percent when bequests were included. The resulting cost-effectiveness ratios show the importance of institutional loyalty and commitment evident in agreements reported by both Grinnell and Wellesley in which the terms were so obviously favorable to the institution.

These factors influenced cultivation costs as well, as discussed in chapter 6. Agreement maintenance costs, on the other hand, seemed to vary with the volume of agreements under management. That is, the total cost of administering agreements does appear to remain relatively flat over a wide range of amounts, of both dollars and agreements, as had been noted in the Ernst & Whinney study report, section 4.2 (see appendix A). The more agreements an institution has in force, the lower the unit cost for agreement maintenance is likely to be. Pomona's cost of 0.5¢ per dollar can be compared to roughly 1.3¢ per dollar at Wellesley and almost 3¢ per dollar for the low-dollar programs (gift annuity and pooled fund) at Grinnell. Grinnell's costs for the entire program are substantially lower when separately managed trusts are included. As more agreements are added to the Wellesley and Grinnell pool of agreements, the cost per dollar will no doubt drop.

What became readily apparent in reviewing the analytical method was that the overall results were extremely sensitive to two factors: the way in which total agreement costs were allocated among the various agreement types, and the average age of the individuals who were to receive income.

This was particularly striking in Grinnell's data, which initially showed an estimated allocation of administration costs of 15 percent to gift annuities and 10 percent to pooled fund agreements. As conservative as these estimates appeared at first glance, the shortcut analytical procedure showed both gift annuities and pooled funds to be of only marginal benefit to Grinnell. What is possible, of course, is that the estimate of costs (an estimate based on the judgment of development officers, as was the case at Pomona) may have been inaccurate. If only 5 percent of the maintenance costs had been allocated to each of the two agreement types, and 90 percent to the trusts, the internal rates of return for both would have been substantially more beneficial. The significance of these results is the demonstrated use of this method to pinpoint program areas of questionable cost effectiveness.

In a similar fashion, the Grinnell results for its gift annuity program depended on the average age of the annuitants. The Grinnell staff had used the oldest age available in table 6.2.2 (E&W Report), consistent with the instructions they had received. However, the difference between an average age of 87 in the Grinnell experience and age 77 in the Ernst & Whinney table could have accounted for large discrepancies in the benefit flow. That is, releases from the Grinnell agreements were projected at a much slower rate than would be expected from a group of very much older annuitants.

What is more, the Ernst & Whinney analysts upon being consulted had thoughts that the shortcut method, already a rough approximation, might be inappropriate for handling very short life expectancies. This uncertainty was magnified when it was learned that only ten gift annuity agreements were involved. With only a small number of agreements, the age of just one or two annuitants could distort the weighted average age to a considerable degree. The lesson to be learned from this experience is that the accuracy of analytical results must be considered suspect when only a few agreements are in effect and the average age of income beneficiaries departs substantially from the Ernst & Whinney range of expected ages.

In comparing the results from the three colleges, it became clear that the choice of agreement types to be offered, or at least emphasized, in a deferred giving program depends on the constituents to be served. Factors, such as the average age of beneficiaries, the amounts to be contributed, and the individual donor's sense of institutional loyalty as a motivating factor, will determine the volume of activity and the nature of the deferred giving agreements. It was not surprising that the programs at Grinnell and Wellesley, although younger in their development, showed significantly better cost-benefit ratios than the more experienced program at Pomona, attributable without doubt to the stronger institutional commitment of their donors.

A further comparison among institutions was made possible by considering an additional analysis performed not as a part of this study effort but which had previously come to our attention. In a 1979 independent study by the Harvard Management Company, the deferred giving program at Harvard University was examined. The purpose of the Harvard self-study was to determine what emphasis ought to be placed on its nascent program as Harvard began its $250 million campaign. In less than five years during which Harvard actively pursued such gifts, excluding bequests, its dollar volume grew from almost $250,000 in 1974 to $6 million in 1977. The study recognized the fact that from the day a donor made a gift to the day the first income payment was made, "an elaborate set of tasks in a long administrative process will occur, involving four separate offices and more than 15 Harvard employees. The offices include those of Planned Giving, the Harvard Treasurer, the Recording Secretary and Harvard Management Company."

The tasks were divided into four categories: booking the gift, accounting and control, managing the investment, and distributing the income. Harvard discovered by a simple time study of the Treasurer's office that individually managed trusts were more expensive to process by a ratio of 2.75 to 1, but they also found that pooled fund gifts, on a one-year budget analysis of the offices of Planned Giving, Recording Secretary, and Treasurer, were 1.8 times as expensive as trusts.

The revenue side, referring only to fair market dollar volume of gift receipts, showed that trust gifts averaged 3.75 times the dollar value of gifts to pooled funds.

The Harvard study took on the issue of outright versus deferred gift by mathematically determining what fraction of the deferred gift might have been given outright. Using a discount factor of 9 percent, which was then the best estimate of Harvard's cost of capital, the study concluded that Harvard's break-even point for $1 of deferred gift was a 35¢ outright gift (i.e., a $10,000 deferred gift was the equivalent of a $3,500 outright gift). Accordingly, the litmus test was: "With every deferred dollar we raise we can ask the question: 'Would 35¢ or more have come in outright funds?'" Harvard's answer: "From our own practical experience, the answer will rarely be 'yes.'"

The comparative test results reveal useful insights into the programs analyzed. The tests also show that the shortcut method may be used to make a reasonable estimate of the internal rate of return for a deferred giving program within certain limits. This conclusion is based on the results from only two institutions. More evidence would be needed to increase the confidence level. One of the significant findings that has been learned from the tests is how difficult it is for even experienced development organizations and business offices to make use of the shortcut method. With this conclusion, the search for a simple and quick method for evaluating deferred giving programs was directed toward a third analytical tool: *procedures for evaluating gift acceptance criteria.* In doing so, we capitalized on the knowledge that the duration of the agreement management period is the single factor that in most instances will drastically affect program profitability.

Criteria for Acceptance of Deferred Gifts

What are the rules?

To find a simpler and less time-consuming method for evaluating the cost–benefit relationship in a deferred giving program, the study directors consulted with Harry A. Turner, Associate Director of Finance, Stanford University. Turner had earlier devised a framework for establishing minimum acceptance criteria for deferred giving agreements to Stanford to achieve a selected benefit objective. This approach is especially useful for the evaluation of deferred giving programs that have started very recently and consequently have accumulated little experience data to arrive at reliable averages such as required in the Ernst & Whinney methods. It will also assist those who are about to start up a program. Turner graciously agreed to update and generalize his analytical method.

Turner's method is not intended to evaluate the return on investment in other than a very general sense. His purpose is to provide a tool by which charitable institutions can have a high degree of assurance that deferred giving agreements will be beneficial. Necessarily, Turner differs from the Ernst & Whinney approaches in several important respects:

1. Turner uses a point estimate for life expectancies of life income beneficiaries, whereas Ernst & Whinney use fractional releases of agreement principal for each year of the projection.
2. Turner states his institutional objective in terms of a minimum

remainder value, while Ernst & Whinney use the internal rate of return calculation to describe profitability.

3. Turner projects unchanging economic factors over the forecast period as compared to the Ernst & Whinney use of econometric projections of inflation rates and market yields on a year-to-year basis. The Turner method can, of course, assume variable economic conditions that may exist at the time of analysis, but it does not provide for annual variations over the management period.

The Turner method is described in the remaining sections of this chapter.

Concept and Guidelines

Whether or not they are stated explicitly, certain expectations for deferred giving programs will have to be adopted by the institution. Generally speaking, gifts will be sought for only those uses that fit the institutional needs. In every case, the development officer will want to design a gift agreement that will show a benefit for the institution rather than a loss.

Three objectives that will define expectations are: 1) the types of agreements to offer to donors; 2) The minimum acceptable level of purchasing power valued when the charitable remainder is to be distributed at the termination of an agreement; 3) The means used to recover acquisition costs (i.e., cultivation and solicitation) as well as agreement maintenance costs while the agreement is under management.

The types of agreements that may be offered to prospective donors consist of gift annuities, pooled income funds, and separately managed trusts (subdivided for this analysis into unitrusts and annuity trusts), all of which have been described in detail elsewhere in this report. From a financial and legal standpoint, gift annuities place the institution at risk because the agreement is designed to invade principal and all of the assets of the institution are pledged against the promise to pay the annuity. In the case of charitable remainder trusts and pooled income funds, only the principal placed in trust is at risk.

Income, used here to describe the variety of payments available from these agreements, is paid to the designated beneficiaries for their lifetimes or a designated term of years, unless at an earlier date the trust assets should be exhausted and the trust consequently terminated. If the assets are exhausted as a result of unfortunate investment selections or of the need to invade principal to make the required annual payments, a question of prudence on the part of the trustee might possibly be raised.

One additional factor for consideration in making these choices is the fact that the rules governing trust assets are different from the rules an institution may follow in managing the property obtained in exchange for a gift annuity agreement. This difference may make it easier to accept certain assets for gift annuity agreements rather than for trusts. Furthermore, it is possible to reinsure gift annuities with commercial insurance companies, making a discounted gift amount available immediately to the charitable organization and displacing the risk.

The Size of the Charitable Remainder

During inflationary times, retention of the entire gift principal can still result in the receipt of a charitable remainder with a substantially diminished purchasing power. For example, receipt of a $100,000 deferred gift that is restricted to field research in biology would be worth only $50,000 after eight years of 9 percent inflation. The prospect of price inflation requires the charitable institution to consider its objectives for the purchasing power of the charitable remainder.

There is a community of interest among the income beneficiaries of deferred gift agreements and the charitable remainderman. In the extreme, if there were no philanthropic intent, the beneficiaries would like to see the principal entirely consumed. The remainderman would prefer the purchasing power of the remainder to be sustained, or possibly increased.

This potential conflict is resolved during the gift acquisition process. Thereafter, the trustee, who is frequently the remainderman, accepts responsibility for the stewardship of the assets according to the terms of the donative agreement.

As a fiduciary, the institution acting as trustee is required to attach equal importance to the income payee's interest and to the remainderman's interest. An institution which under a single agreement is both remainderman and trustee must devote meticulous attention to the interests of the income beneficiary to avoid any appearance that self-interest is influencing trustee decisions. These competing interests are compromised when the agreement is set up by mutually working out the income payment rate the beneficiaries will receive.

The income payment rates are discretionary within limits set by revenue codes and regulations for charitable remainder gifts that qualify for tax benefits. Many institutions are guided in their gift annuity plans by the rate schedule adopted by the Committee on Gift Annuities. Trusts more often than not are planned to preserve the original principal amount.

The objective, then, is to define the desired level of purchasing power of the remainder. The relevant rate of inflation for this consideration is the cost rise of prospective use of the gift (e.g., field research in biology). A good measure to use for all gifts is the prospective rate of cost rise in the charitable institution's operating budget. Since a typical operating budget is labor intensive (that is, most of it is allocated to wages and benefits), it can be expected to inflate at about the same rate as labor costs. Labor costs inflate faster than general price inflation, about 2 percent per year faster. Gift principal can be expected to lose purchasing power faster than the erosive effects of general price inflation.

Purchasing power of the charitable remainder can be sustained, or even increased, in two ways: 1) in the form of retained capital gains, and 2) in the form of income which is capitalized. Income is capitalized when the income earned through investment of the assets in an agreement exceeds the amount of income which must be paid out. The undistributed income is reinvested with the principal in the agreement.

Disbursement Policy

The basic question regarding purchasing power of the remainder is whether it should increase, decrease, or stay the same. The payout rate is determined by the answer to this question. The disbursement policy that corresponds to the objective for the remainder is called "positive" (increase purchasing power), "negative," or "neutral."

The total return to an investment consists of price gain or loss and income. If bonds are acquired at par and held until they mature, their return will consist entirely of income. In the case of common stocks paying a dividend and of bonds acquired at a price above or below par, the return will consist of income and of capital gains or losses. In general, high yield stocks have reduced prospects for capital gains, and conversely, low yield stocks increase prospects for capital gains.

If the entire total return were disbursed in the form of payout, the initial gift principal would be preserved but it would lose purchasing power during inflationary times. In fact, purchasing power could be sustained only if the portion of the total return *in excess of inflation* were disbursed. This neutral disbursement policy would pay out only the "real" portion of the total return, and it would retain and reinvest the inflationary portion. Moreover, a neutral disbursement policy would also sustain the purchasing power of the payout. During a period of 5 percent inflation and 10 percent total return, a neutral disbursement policy would pay out only the return in excess of inflation, 5 percent. This policy would cause the size of the assets and of the payout to increase at a rate that would exactly offset inflation. The example contained in table 8.1 shows principal and payout increasing by the rate of inflation, 5 percent per year.

A negative disbursement policy would pay out more than the "real" portion of the total return. The effect of paying out a portion of the inflationary return is to lose purchasing power of both the principal and the payout. During a period of 6 percent inflation and 10 percent real return, a payout of 7 percent would cause purchasing power to be lost at the rate of 3 percent per year. An example of this negative disburse-

Table 8.1. Neutral Disbursement Policy

Year	Principal Value	Total Return	Payout	Reinvested Return
1	$100	$10.00	$5.00	$5.00
2	105	10.50	5.25	5.25
3	110.25	11.03	5.52	5.51

ment policy is contained in table 8.2. In this case, principal and payout are increasing by only 3 percent per year, less than the rate of inflation.

The implementation of a disbursement policy, given a set of expectations for investment performance, requires merely a maximum allowable payout rate. These expectations certainly will be specific and unique to each charitable institution, but certain applicable observations about classes of investment media, e.g., domestic stocks and bonds, will be helpful.

Theories of capital markets generally agree that total returns to stocks and bonds should exceed general price inflation over the long term. Empirical evaluations of historical returns do show real returns but with substantial, occasionally persistent, deviations from expectations over a period of many years. Currently the ranges of these expectations are:

Investment	Expected Annual Real Return
Stocks	6 to 10%
Bonds	1 to 4%

With respect to expected rates of dividend income there is no theory, just empirical observation. During the last decade,

Table 8.2. Negative Disbursement Policy

Return	Initial Principal	Total Return	Payout	Reinvested Return
1	$100	$10.00	$7.00	$3.00
2	103	10.30	7.21	3.09
3	106.09	10.61	7.43	3.18

the dividend yield to the Standard and Poors Index of 500 common stocks has varied between a bit under 3 percent and 5.5 percent.

Cost Analysis

It is important that institutions give careful thought to how acquisition costs and agreement maintenance costs are to be paid. They must be paid by the institution itself or by the donor.

If agreement maintenance costs or, less commonly, acquisition costs are to be paid for by the donor, there are several options. The agreement itself can call for the payment of a management fee—this would apply to agreements other than gift annuities. Management fees are chargeable to principal or income accounts as specified by state codes or in some states as agreed to by the trustor and trustee.

A second option is to require that the size of the gift be sufficiently large to cover the cumulative cost of the maintenance costs. Unlike an endowment gift or an expendable gift, the deferred gift provides no current financial benefit to the charitable organization. When the charitable organization meets its responsibilities without fee, deferred gifts incur management expenses that are not offset by the investment return to the assets. Therefore, the charitable organization is worse off financially during the period prior to receipt of the remainder. The purpose of having a minimum acceptable gift policy is to attempt to assure that the charitable organization's costs will be recovered and that there will be a net remaining gift.

The outright expendable gift for the purpose of offsetting the prospective maintenance costs is a third way to assure that the receipt of the deferred gift will make the institution better off. In this case, principal and the entire investment return might be used to pay costs. Because of these characteristics, the size of the outright gift requirement usually will be less than the size of the minimum acceptable gift.

Whatever the source of expense payment, whether it be the

institution or the donor, the essential distinction for the determination of gift acceptance guidelines is whether or not the maintenance costs are to be recovered by annual cash payments. If costs are covered by annual cash payments from the institution's operating budget, from an outright expendable gift, or from the payment of management fees by the trust, then the guidelines merely are the disbursement policies.

If costs are to be recovered from the remainder, then policies for minimum acceptable gifts are to be added to the guidelines. The underlying concept is that the remainder should be at least large enough to offset the cumulative value of the annual management costs.

Preparation of Acceptance Criteria

The steps to be followed in preparing a table showing the acceptance criteria in minimum acceptable combinations are these:

1. Describe the minimum acceptable remainder value, taking into consideration purchasing power, cumulative costs that may have to be offset, and designated uses.
2. Estimate acquisition costs and agreement maintenance costs. Decide how to allocate costs to individual agreements.
3. Calculate the management period, using mortality tables to estimate life expectancies of the payees.
4. Make capital market assumptions that will assign investment yields as well as total return on investments.
5. Choose an investment mix that is appropriate to the level of income payments.
6. Calculate minimum gift sizes, valued at the time an agreement is to be set up.

The desired remainder value can be stated as: a percentage of costs, a percentage of the original principal amount, a fixed dollar amount above costs, or a combination of these alternatives. The type of guideline that would be useful in considering remainder values are illustrated below:

The payout percentage for deferred gifts cannot exceed an amount that would reasonably be expected to cause the assets to lose purchasing power at a rate in excess of 2 percent per year. Currently, this maximum percentage is 9 percent.

A life income gift to be held and managed without charge is acceptable only if the prospective remainder exceeds the cumulative value of the fund's future management costs.

Cost estimation involves agreement maintenance costs, such as services to beneficiaries, e.g., tax advice, investment portfolio summary reports, bookkeeping, check preparation, postal charges, bank custodial services, investment management, and perhaps legal fees. These costs are likely to vary among the types of agreement that are offered.

Unitrusts usually have the largest maintenance costs. Each payment may be accompanied by a lengthy, comprehensive report. Investment transactions normally involve research, brokerage, and letter reports to beneficiaries. Fiduciary tax returns prepared by the trustee are lengthy. In contrast, a single tax return is filed for a pooled income fund. Beneficiaries of pooled income fund agreements may be advised at the end of the year of all the investment transactions for the prior twelve months. The annual agreement maintenance costs reported by those institutions that submitted cost data for this study seem to fall within the range of 0.5 to 1.5 percent of the fair market value of the assets under management. As shown in chapter 7, however, these costs are projected to inflate over twenty years to an annual level of 3 percent. A typical compilation of cost information might be as shown in table 8.3.

Estimating the number of years that an agreement will have to be managed depends on actuarial forecasts. Ernst & Whinney selected a mortality table in use by the insurance industry to fit to the Pomona College population of donors and beneficiaries. By and large, individuals who purchase annuities from insurance companies and individuals who establish charitable remainder agreements appear to have significantly longer life expectancies than indicated by mortality tables

Table 8.3 Compilation of Cost Information

	Unitrusts	Annuity Trusts	Pooled Income Fund
Trust services	$696	$376	$ 46
Bookkeeping	56	56	24
Custodial services	32	32	12
Investment management	16	16	118 + % of assets
Total dollars per Agreement	$800	$480	$200 + % of assets

which apply to the entire population of the country. It would be prudent to consult an actuary to obtain an informed estimate of life expectancies for a special constituency.

The assumptions to be made with respect to capital market factors during the management period are of critical importance. Only imperfect theories exist for projecting these values. The factors to be considered in any such forecast would include:

> General price inflation
>
> Total real return, stocks
>
> Total real return, bonds
>
> Yield, stocks
>
> Yield, bonds

These factors will be used to determine an approximate investment mix and to evaluate the disbursement policy. For example, consider this set of expectations:

Inflation	9%
Total real return, stocks	9%
Yield to stocks	5%
Total real return, bonds	3%
Yield to bonds	12%

If only income is to be paid out and a neutral disbursement policy is desired, payment cannot exceed the total real return to stocks—in this case, 9 percent. However, since stocks provide only 5 percent in income, some higher yielding bonds must be added to the investment mix to increase income. The introduction of bonds to the mix causes the total return to be less than that from stocks alone. As shown in table 8.4, a neutral disbursement policy is achieved with a mix that is roughly 70 percent stocks (yielding 5 percent in dividends) and 30 percent bonds (yielding 12 percent in interest payments). As is evident, payments which exceed 7 percent fall into the negative disbursement area and payouts which are below 7 percent are positive. In practice, most institutions will find it necessary to adopt a negative disbursement policy to attract donors. A negative disbursement policy of 2 percent per year corresponds to a 9 percent payment rate which would result in a loss of purchasing power of 18 percent of the principal in each ten-year period while under management.

In the example above, the stock yield plays a key role in setting the investment mix. Utility common stocks, which are sensitive to interest rates, have been yielding 12 percent or more in recent years. Would it be possible to accept a gift of shares of a utility common stock yielding 12 percent and agree to pay 10 percent without violating the disbursement policy? No, it would not because high yielding stocks have a lower appreciation potential and consequently a less favorable total return.

Minimum Acceptable Gifts

To illustrate how all of these factors are brought together to prepare a table that will specify minimum gift size as related to the terms of the agreement, consider a unitrust with an 84-year-old male donor-payee. The expected duration of the management period is five years. Suppose that a cost study has established that the annual management costs of the unitrust are $800. Suppose also that a rate of 9 percent inflation is expected to prevail, so that the prospective rate of cost rise of management costs is 11 percent per year.

With these assumptions, the annual burden on the fund sources for the operating budget will rise to $1,214 during the

Table 8.4. Investment Mix and Disbursement Policy

	Disbursement Policy										
	Negative					Neutral			Positive		
Stock %	0	10	20	30	40	50	60	70	80	90	100
Bond %	100	90	80	70	60	50	40	30	20	10	0
Real return %	3.0	3.6	4.2	4.8	5.4	6.0	6.6	7.2	7.8	8.4	9.0
Yield %	12	11.3	10.6	9.9	9.2	8.5	7.8	7.1	6.4	5.7	5.0

Table 8.5. Computation of Minimum Acceptable Gift

Assumptions: First year management cost: $800
Rate of cost rise: 11%

Year	Cost (11% compound)	Foregone Value After Fifth Year (11% compound)
1	$ 800	$1,348
2	888	1,348
3	986	1,348
4	1094	1,348
5	1214	1,348
	Minimum acceptable remainder	$6,740

Table 8.6. Minimum Acceptable Unitrust Gifts with Five year Holding Period

Percent Unitrust	Minimum Acceptable Gift
7	$4237
8	4717
9	5133

fifth year. Moreover, each annual payment forgoes an opportunity to make an investment, either financial or in some other program benefit. The cumulative cost at the end of five years is $6,740. It is this cost which the remainder should exceed if the deferred gift is to benefit the charitable institution (table 8.5).

What size gift can be expected to produce the minimum acceptable remainder? The size of the gift is determined by the total investment return that it is expected to be realized during the holding period and by the portion of the total return that is disbursed to the beneficiary. In the case of an 8 percent unitrust, the expected total return will exceed the assumed 9 percent inflation by 6.4 percent. After the 8 percent disbursement has been made the net rate of increase in value will be 7.4 percent. The minimum acceptable gift, then, is the one that will increase in size to $6,740 after five years of growth at 7.4 percent per year. A compound interest calculation shows this amount to be $4,717.

Other minimum acceptable gifts, all required to produce the same minimum acceptable remainder, for different percentage unitrusts are shown in table 8.6. Note the tradeoff between the payout percentage and the size of the minimum acceptable gift: increases in the payout require increases in the size of the minimum acceptable gift.

The final step requires the development of a financial model of each kind of life income gift, given the results of the prior steps. Portions of the resulting tables would appear as in table 8.7. The entries in table 8.7 demonstrate that the size of the minimum acceptable gift increases rapidly as the payout rate increases. However, the upper limit to payout rates contained in the table is set by the charitable institution's disbursement policy. They also demonstrate that increases in the holding period cause sharp increases in the minimum acceptable gift size, with the possible exception of annuity trusts. This interesting exception for annuity trusts arises because the fixed dollar payout becomes a smaller proportion (percentage) of the trust assets as their value increases. This subsequent reduction in the payout percentage permits the investment manager to increase the stock proportion of the mix, thereby in-

Table 8.7. Minimum Acceptable Life Income Gifts
(dollar figures in thousands)

Expected Duration (years)	One Beneficiary Age F	One Beneficiary Age M	Two Beneficiaries (male and female, male two years older; male age shown)	Pooled Income Fund	Unitrust Pay-out rate 5%	7%	9%	11%	Annuity Trust Pay-out rate 5%	7%	9%	11%
0 to 5	86 or over	84 or over	94 or over	$ 1	$ 4	$ 4	$ 5	$ 6	$2	$3	$ 3	$ 4
6 to 10	77–85	74–83	84–93	3	7	9	13	19	3	5	7	11
11 to 15	70–76	65–73	77–83	5	9	15	25	44	4	6	10	20
16 to 20	64–69	58–64	70–76	8	11	22	43	90	4	7	12	32
21 to 25	59–63	52–57	65–69	11	13	29	70	174	4	7	14	43
26 to 30	53–58	47–51	59–64	15	14	38	107	322	4	7	15	53
31 to 35	48–52	41–46	54–58	20	15	48	160	578	4	7	15	61
36 to 40	43–47	36–40	49–53	27	16	59	235	1019	4	7	15	66
41 to 45	38–42	31–35	44–48	35	16	72	340	1767	4	7	15	69
46 to 50	32–37	26–30	39–43	45	16	87	484	3026	4	7	15	72

creasing its expected rate of growth. On the other hand, an annuity trust can be very troublesome if, for any reason, the trust income should decline, requiring the trustee thereby to invade the trust principal to make the fixed annual payments. The snowballing effect can soon erode the earning power of the trust assets past the point of recovery.

How to Apply the Method

The preparation of a table of minimum acceptable gift size can be accomplished by charitable organizations which are inexperienced in managing deferred giving programs as well as those that have decades of experience. Every organization faces the same uncertain future in selecting values for factors that must be estimated, whether they be econometric factors or life expectancy estimates. The experienced organization can have more confidence in applying costs that are based on actual experience. However, the cost values appear to be reasonably consistent among the more experienced institutions from which data was obtained. An organization considering a deferred giving program for the first time could rely on those cost estimates without fear of being too far wrong.

The table of minimum acceptable gift size is an excellent means of involving the governing board of the charitable organization in the decision-making process and the goal-setting procedures that are necessary both for new deferred giving programs as well as those that are ongoing. Once such a table has been approved by the trustees or regents, the development staff can proceed confidently to offer gift agreements that satisfy the minimum requirements. There will, of course, be exceptions. The donor whose initial gift is smaller than required may intend to make a series of such gifts, the total of which will exceed the minimum. Perhaps a provision in the donor's will for a bequest to the institution would be the basis for asking for an exception. In making exceptions, the important point is to require the approval of the governing board to permit an evaluation of risk and to make the board aware of the number of exceptions which have been recommended by the staff.

While the numerical results obtained from the use of this method must be regarded as very rough estimates, it is a most useful tool for comparing alternative acceptance criteria and for weighing the possible effects of sharp changes in econometric factors during extended management periods.

NINE

Processing and Managing Charitable Remainder Gifts and Annuities

A second and third step.

If the importance of agreement management has not been sufficiently clear before, this study should leave no doubt of the
crucial part played by trust administrators and business officers in deferred giving programs. The need to satisfy the institution's legal obligations when serving in a fiduciary role
should be easily recognized. Beyond this, the cultivation of
donors who have already made contributions has been discussed in chapter 4. The importance of "repeat" donors varies
from institution to institution, but a donor who has confidence
in the administrator's professional competence and feels a
warm personal relationship with the staff is an excellent prospect. Now it is quite evident that the value of the benefits the
university will eventually receive from a trust or annuity
agreement will depend to a considerable extent on the agreement maintenance costs and the success of the investment
program. In the past, it has been all too easy to place too much
emphasis on the marketing and cultivation aspects of deferred
giving and too little on agreement maintenance.

In the literature of fundraising and in the classrooms of
seminars on planned giving, there are abundant opportunities
to learn the whys and wherefores of deferred gifts. A sample
seminar includes such topics as:

—Starting and implementing an effective planned giving program

—Estate planning approach to planned giving

—The tools of planned giving

—Building a viable prospect list

—Guidelines and practical considerations in funding planned gifts

—Effective promotional techniques in planned giving

—Income, gift, and estate tax aspects of inter vivos charitable remainder trusts

Rarely do such programs delve into the nitty-gritty of what to do after the gift is secured.

The Pomona study divided costs into two categories: 1) cultivation and solicitation costs; and 2) agreement maintenance costs (see appendix A, E&W Report, section 3.3.4).

This may seem an arbitrary division of costs which neglects the cost of additional cultivation after the first agreement has been signed by a donor. The more important question is what it takes to induce a satisfied donor to make an additional gift to the same college or university. Cost-effective management of the agreement and above-average investment results have already been mentioned. Above all, personal attention and interest in the donor will inspire feelings of confidence in the deferred giving program and of admiration for the institution that lead to follow-on gifts.

Knowing then that acquisition costs are fixed—for they cease to be measured when the gift agreement is executed—and maintenance costs will be extended for the life of the agreement, critical attention to the management function is called for. It has not however become the subject matter of examination, discussion, and refinement as has the marketing process. The ultimate dollar value of a charitable remainder gift to a charitable institution will generally rise or fall with the correctness and skill with which that gift is processed, managed and invested from the date it starts to the date it finishes.

In many charitable institutions and particularly in colleges and universities, it is the financial officers that are the bellwethers of economizing. They are accordingly loath to enforce budget cuts elsewhere without exercising exemplary self-restraint in their own departments. When it comes to managing planned gifts, the tender loving care required bespeaks self-interest and, across-the-board budget cuts, however else effective, will often be counterproductive in this area. It is more than self-interest, however, that suggests the need for excellence in management. Accountability as a fiduciary to a life-income beneficiary is a serious legal responsibility, made even more compelling where the charity is both trustee and charitable remainderman.

To introduce the functions requires attention to the legend of the stonecutters as told by Peter Drucker, the father of the concept of management by objective. Three such artisans were at work one day when a curious passerby stopped and asked each of them what they were doing.

> The first replied: "I am making a living." The second kept on hammering while he said: "I am doing the best job of stonecutting in the entire country." The third one looked up with a visionary gleam in his eyes and said: 'I am building a cathedral.'"

Banks, trust companies, investment counselors, real estate managers, life insurance companies, all respectably engaged in profit-making enterprises, establish their charges to produce a suitable profit after expenses. Few nonprofit institutions have the capacity to apply those principles to the management of planned gifts, either by choice or by lack of ability to do so. Whether or not profit is the most appropriate term to use in connection with a gift program, the obvious requirement is that gifts be accepted which enhance the financial status of the institution rather than sapping the institution's resources.

To build the "cathedral" of endowment there may be no single formula of success but to the financial artisans to whom this task falls we urge new care and attention. Farming out the responsibility is not wholly possible when one examines the functions to be performed and we describe those functions hereafter to suggest the application of thoughtful cost considerations to each of them as well as to all of them.

In appendix C, an outline developed at the University of

Pennsylvania discusses the internal procedures and responsibilities involved in accepting and processing a deferred gift agreement. A full understanding of the plan's efficiency requires some knowledge of the organizational relationships at the University of Pennsylvania.

The development department had two organizational components for this purpose, the Office of Planned Giving and the Office of Counsel to the development program. The process of gift acquisition and solicitation followed by stewardship fell to the Office of Planned Giving, which included a Life Income Trust Officer, and the legal and tax ramifications were the responsibility of the Office of Counsel, which exercised the right to call in outside counsel when needed. The Office of the Treasurer served as the repository of all university assets, including trust assets and the receipt and disbursement of all university funds.

Through the ranks of financial heirarchy to the Vice President for Finance, the investments of the university were under the control of an investment board, chaired by a trustee but composed of experts in several fields of investments including securities. This board also had the say in determining the use of investment counselors and custodians. Finally, there was an ad hoc Trustee Committee on Planned Gifts that had general oversight of all of the program, including both the development and financial aspects.

Over the four-year period from 1976 to 1979, the university received in excess of $35 million in its planned giving programs, of which more than $20 million were bequests and over $13 million were inter vivos charitable remainder agreements. The successful processing of this volume of activity depended to a great degree on the step-by-step implementation of the outline. The careful collection of information about the settlor prior to settlement, the checks and balances by the participation of several organizational segments, and the attention given to providing the settlor with prompt and accurate reports merged in forming an image of a highly professional and caring program.

It is not the purpose or intention of this report to furnish a detailed functional guide. Nonetheless, to the issue of cost effectiveness there must be directed some attention to what will entail costs. Charitable remainder life income agreement maintenance is not a simple process. At least the same degree of reliance upon a successful gift program is warranted by a successful agreement maintenance program. A variety of skills and talents challenges the administrator of such a program and full cognizance by the governing board is essential from the very beginning.

There is a tendency in charitable organizations to specialize—particularly in our colleges and universities where academicians often set the management pace. In treating planned giving as a specialty, the trustees may not be serving the best interests of the institution. In *Management Focus*, Charles A. Nelson spoke again of Peter Drucker when he referred to the recognizable analogies in the university to Drucker's caution to the business enterprise:

> This striving for professional workmanship in functional and specialized work is also a danger. It tends to direct a man's vision and efforts away from the goals of the business.
>
> The functional work becomes an end in itself. In far too many instances the functional manager no longer measures his performance by its contribution to the enterprise, but only by his own professional criteria of workmanship. He tends to appraise his subordinates by their craftsmanship, to reward and promote them accordingly . . .
>
> The functional manager's legitimate desire for workmanship becomes, unless counterbalanced, a centrifugal force which tears the enterprise apart and converts it into a loose confederation of functional empires, each concerned only with its own craft, each jealously guarding its own "secrets," each bent on enlarging its own domain rather than on building the business.

No one who has spent time as an administrator at a college suggests that an educational institution should be run like a business. Nonetheless, where there are functions such as trust agreement maintenance or planned gift promotion that do not involve tendentious issues of academic freedom or tenure, there are cost-benefit considerations to which the business community is attuned and colleges are not. The time for change is now.

Conclusions, Questions, and Recommendations

Where to next?

Perspective with regard to charitable giving should not be lost in the isolation of single issues. This report narrowly focuses on the question of *"when is a dollar raised in a deferred gift a dollar gained."* Inherent in any analysis of cost-benefit is a reliance on economic methods applicable to profit-making enterprises. There are, however, limitations in the extension of business practices to nonprofit institutions.

It has been said that through philanthropic giving and receiving, we preserve the process of enlightenment. In this process, the elements of supply and demand are as critical, if not more critical, to the survival of the fittest—a cardinal principle of the free enterprise system. In the next decade, Americans, through their support, will decide which institutions are to survive. The competition for the donative dollar will intensify. Institutional loyalties and commitments to special causes will become sources of conflict in the hearts of the many who will determine the philanthropic priorities.

In a very real way, this process has been going on since the Pilgrims landed, but now our society has become so complex that we need statutes to help us to establish and preserve our social and political priorities. The federal and state tax incentives to charitable giving evidence this concern. To those who would curtail the charitable deduction provisions of the Internal Revenue Code we urge caution.

Tax incentives to charitable giving make possible the diversity and quality in our daily lives. They encourage individual participation in a monumental enterprise which has, among other things, produced: 1) the highest quality post-secondary educational opportunities in the world; 2) a better, more decent, society; 3) enhanced health care and cures; 4) technology competitive with the rest of the world; and 5) quality of life through culture.

The study of cost effectiveness of fundraising serves two basic purposes: first, the contributing public has the right to know where their gift dollars go and how they are spent, and second, the managers of the nonprofit enterprises have the obligation to make the best possible use of those gift dollars.

For the charitable remainder gift programs of nonprofit institutions:

1. The cost effectiveness of deferred giving programs can be estimated using either the Ernst & Whinney procedures or the Turner method described in chapter 8. The uncertainties inherent in forecasting the future are an essential part of the analysis and, therefore, these procedures will prove to be more useful as the means to improve cost effectiveness of a program rather than to calculate an accurate cost-revenue ratio.

2. Despite the said uncertainties, the time-consuming efforts necessary to collect data and to perform the arithmetic calculations are worthwhile. The entire data retrieval and computation process focuses management attention on: a) institutional cost controls; b) the validity of minimum gift acceptance criteria; c) the type of deferred giving agreements which should or should not be offered; and d) the desired benefit level which the institution wishes to achieve.

3. While close working relationships between development officers and business officers are important in operating a cost-effective deferred giving program, the study results show clearly that it is the trust management (agreement maintenance) function that is the key to financial success. The annual maintenance costs, measured in terms of dollars under management, and portfolio investment results are the vital factors in determining the real value of the remainder to the institution. Furthermore, both factors exert a strong influence in encouraging donors to make repeat gifts.

4. Donor motivation plays a significant part in determining the cost effectiveness of a deferred giving program. Pomona's program, based principally on an appeal to individuals with no prior connection to the college produces a good rate of return on costs. These results, however, do not compare to the even more favorable returns realized by Grinnell and Wellesley, which are supported almost exclusively by their graduates and trustees.

5. In disclosing fundraising costs for deferred giving programs, the most accurate and informative presentation is that used by Ernst & Whinney in the cost–benefit analysis (E & W Report, table 4.5.2) i.e., the cultivation and solicitation cost per dollar of agreement in force based on the most recent five years of experience. While this factor does not relate program costs to the present value of the institution's remainder interest, its use avoids the uncertainties which are an intrinsic part of the present value calculation. Furthermore, cultivation and solicitation costs are the most easily explained cost concept for disclosure to the public.

Fundraising will always be more an art than a science. Charitable institutions, no matter what the impact of technology may be, will still need a convincing raison d'être to achieve their goals. As primarily service organizations they will always be labor cost intensive. Efficiency in management will be indispensable to their solvency and success. Donor relations will always require a high level of time and attention by development officers and their supervisors and institutional credibility must be carefully nurtured and protected. In the relationship created by a gift subject to a life or a term interest, the charitable institution has a higher duty than self-perpetuation; it has a fiduciary responsibility to which faithful and competent adherence must prevail.

It is the common hope of the many who participated in and supported this research project that this report will serve the philanthropic community in attaining these high levels of obligation in a more professional manner than has been available hitherto.

APPENDIX A

The Ernst & Whinney Report

Ernst & Whinney

515 S. Flower Street
Los Angeles, California 90071
213/621-1666

September 30, 1980

Mr. William H. Dunseth
Special Assistant to the President
and Counsel for Development
Pomona College

Mr. Norman S. Fink
Vice President, Development and University Relations
Brandeis University

Mr. Howard C. Metzler
Director, Annuity and Trust Program
Pomona College

Gentlemen:

We have completed our assignment to conduct a COST/BENEFIT
ANALYSIS OF THE POMONA PLAN. Our report is presented
following this summary letter.

Our study was undertaken to evaluate the costs and benefits of
the deferred giving fund raising programs at Pomona College. This
evaluation consists of two major tasks:

1. To develop a methodology for analyzing the costs and
   benefits of deferred giving fund raising programs using, as
   the basis for the methodology, the historical data and
   experience of Pomona College.

2. To present the findings resulting from the application of this
   methodology to the deferred giving program at Pomona
   College, herein referred to as the Pomona Plan.

The report consists of three principal sections:

1. Engagement Approach
2. Engagement Findings
3. Appendices

The Engagement Approach section presents a detailed topical
review of our approach to executing the study. The Engagement
Findings section presents a review of our findings from each
phase of the work. The Appendices contain the detailed statistical
and financial data which support the findings.

To promote a clearer understanding of this report, we have, with your assistance, included a section in which certain frequently used terms are defined.

This study has required the extension of the theories of modern financial analysis to deferred giving fund raising programs. A review of the literature has failed to locate any prior studies of this nature. With regard to the findings presented herein, several important clarifications are warranted:

1. The methodology for preparing cost and benefit analyses for deferred giving fund raising programs, whether college and university based or some other form of organization, is expected to be of general applicability to most charitable institutions. It will be noted that the methods require reasonably comprehensive accounting records with regard to historical costs and agreements in force. Charitable institutions with established accounting and agreement record keeping systems should find their records sufficient to support the methodology.

2. The methods presented in this report will be of only partial value to the institution seeking to establish a deferred giving program for the first time. The specific methodology requires an existing body of historical data and does not provide any guidance in anticipating new deferred gifts. However, the discussion of the technical issues which is presented in this report should be very useful in conducting a thorough review of the economic issues related to establishing a new deferred giving program. Further, it may be possible to use the methodology to prepare projections of the prospective performance of a new deferred giving program which would be useful in the decision to establish such a program.

It is important to note that the findings of this report as they relate to the costs and benefits of the Pomona Plan—the second major task of this assignment—depend to a large extent on the actual facts and circumstances as they prevail at Pomona College. The most significant of these facts and circumstances are:

1. Pomona College has traditionally sought gifts from outside its "family" members—trustees, faculty, administrative staff, students and their families, and alumni. This policy was a condition of establishing the program. In seeking gifts from the general public, marketing techniques are used which incur costs which are likely to be quite dissimilar from those of other colleges and universities but quite similar to other public charities without such constituencies.

2. Pomona College is actively involved in managing the assets held in connection with deferred gifts. The College makes investment policy and engages money managers to implement these policies.

3. Pomona College has had a formal deferred giving program since 1946. The program has achieved a level of maturity and sophistication which has been duplicated in very few other charitable institutions.

4. The fund raising focus of the Pomona Plan has been to seek annuity and trust agreements from living donors. The College only recently began a program of actively seeking bequests, and that program is designed to alert and educate the alumni of the College to the opportunities related to bequests in the context of estate planning. The bequest program is not designed to seek these gifts from individuals outside the "family" community. However, the efforts of the College to attract annuity and trust agreements do include, based on the estate planning needs of prospective donors, discussions regarding bequests. To this extent, the bequest program is not strictly related to members of the "family" community.

For these reasons, the findings of this report about the cost and benefit relationships of the Pomona Plan should be viewed as unique to Pomona College. Each charitable institution seeking deferred gifts has policies and procedures which are likely to differ to some degree from their peers. Certainly, therefore, each charitable institution should expect that similar research on their deferred giving fund raising program will produce different findings than those for Pomona College.

We have also prepared a series of work sheets representing a simplified approach to the cost–benefit analysis. They are contained in appendix N. The work sheets may or may not parallel each characteristic of every program type and contractual arrangement. They can, however, be reasonably expected to bear some resemblance to the key attributes of annuity and trust programs at colleges and universities.

The findings of this report are based on a body of assumptions regarding historical costs and future events which are fundamental to any analysis of this sort. We wish to point out that the actual fund raising results achieved by the Pomona Plan or by any deferred giving program over the ensuing years may bear little resemblance to the projections which form the basis of this report. The occurrence of future events is fundamentally uncertain and there can be no assurance that these projections will be achieved.

The findings presented in this report are the result of an evolutionary process which resulted from our mutual growth in understanding and defining the technical environment and the approach to addressing the objectives of this study. We fully expect and anticipate that subsequent study on the economics of deferred giving fund raising programs will further advance this understanding and definition.

The Pomona Plan achieves rates of gift returns which are very attractive in economic terms. It is clear to us that the investment return achieved by the deferred giving programs demonstrates the fundamental economic soundness of these programs.

We are excited about the potential benefits afforded colleges, universities, and other not-for-profit organizations through the application of cost/benefit techniques developed on the Pomona College experience. With serious budgetary constraints facing institutions of higher learning in the future, a deferred giving program appears to afford a real and consistently positive source of cash.

We would be happy to assist in any way we can to either adapt the computerized financial model to a specific facility, prepare donor acceptance criteria, or be of service in any other way.

This engagement has required large commitments of time, skill, and energy from the executives of Pomona College and from yourselves as the principal investigators. The work could not have been completed otherwise. We deeply appreciate this assistance, which has contributed in large measure to the quality of this report.

Very truly yours,

Ernst & Whinney

Contents

SECTION 1

Definition of Terms

ACCEPTANCE CRITERIA: The standards or rules which govern the decision to accept or reject a given gift agreement. Acceptance criteria generally include such considerations as the number of beneficiaries, their age and life expectancy, the nature and value of the assets which make up the gift, the returns expected by the donor, the investment returns achieved and likely to be achieved, and the likelihood of additional subsequent gifts.

AGREEMENT: Each individual gift annuity contract or each pooled fund trust, unitrust or annuity trust created as the result of a gift by a donor.

AGREEMENTS IN FORCE: All agreements involving at least one living income recipient.

AGREEMENT MAINTENANCE: The activities of a deferred giving program related to managing a gift after it has been obtained. These activities include, but are not limited to, gift accounting, investment management, paying and receiving, and donor counseling.

ASSUMPTIONS: Predicted expectations of future policies or performances based on historical performance of costs on the cost side; based on agreements in force as of June 30, 1978, and the terms of those agreements on the revenue side.

BASE CASE: The Internal Rates of Return for gift annuities, pooled funds, and separately managed trusts assuming no change in bond interest rates or stock prices during the twenty-year projection period.

BENEFICIARY: Any individual named in a gift annuity contract or a charitable remainder trust agreement who is now, or may at a future date, receive income payments under the terms of the contract or trust agreement.

CASH FLOWS: Cash receipts earned from interest or dividend income net of the payout required by the contract or the agreement.

CULTIVATION AND SOLICITATION: All of the marketing and promotional efforts related to seeking gifts are included. With respect to any single donor, cultivation and solicitation has been assumed to cease with the signing of a gift agreement.

DEFERRED GIVING: This phrase includes gift annuities, pooled funds, separately managed trusts, and bequests. The report presents a detailed explanation of these forms of gifts as they operate at Pomona College.

DEPARTMENTAL COSTS: The total of that portion of the budget of each department of the College which is involved in supporting the Pomona Plan.

HISTORICAL COST: The cost data contained in the accounting records of Pomona College for the period 1975–1979.

INTERNAL RATE OF RETURN (IRR): The interest rate which equates the present value of the expected future receipts from agreements in force to the costs of obtaining those receipts.

INVESTMENT COUNSELORS: Those who offer advice and counsel to the persons responsible for establishing investment policy and who manage the assets assigned to them by the College.

OUTRIGHT BEQUEST: A bequest in which the gift amount is immediately available for use by the College. This term is used to distinguish these gifts from bequests which establish annuity or trust agreements.

"OUTSIDE" COSTS: Categories of costs in the budget not listed by department, a portion of which can be ascribed to the Pomona Plan (Trust Administration, custodial fees, real estate expenses, for example).

POMONA COLLEGE "FAMILY": Graduates, former students, trustees, faculty; spouses of each; and parents.

POMONA PLAN: The solicitation, receipt, and management of gift annuities, charitable remainder trusts, and bequests.

POOL OF AGREEMENTS: All *Agreements in Force* as of June 30, 1978.

PORTFOLIO MIX: The division between bonds and equities in the deferred giving portfolio.

PORTFOLIO TURNOVER: The replacement of bonds at maturity with similar bonds carrying a new market rate based on the econometric model in use.

RELEASE: The termination of an annuity or trust agreement and the related availability of the remaining principal amount of a gift. The principle amount is sometimes described herein as the corpus.

SECTION 2

The Plans

2.1. The Gift Annuity

The gift annuity is a contract between the institution and the donor. The institution pays a guaranteed lifetime annuity in return for the gift of cash, securities, or real property. The same income may continue to a spouse, a relative, or a friend for life, but there may not be more than two income beneficiaries on each agreement.

In most states, annuities are written in conformity with the insurance code of the state and under supervision of the state Commissioner of Insurance. The rates of return are determined by the ages of the beneficiaries and are lower than comparable rates offered by commercial insurance companies. This difference in rates of return is accounted for by the fact that most charitable organizations expect to have at least 50 percent of the principal contributed as a remainder at the time the last beneficiary dies. The Committee on Gift Annuities, an organization made up of many of the charitable organizations in the United States that issue gift annuities, publishes recommended rates every three years after a study of mortality tables and an analysis of projected investment earnings. Most charities use the rates proposed by the committee. Some, however, take into account their own investment experience to determine the rate they will offer to a donor on an individual gift basis. In any case, the dollar amount of the annual annuity, fixed at the time the contract is written, does not change throughout the existence of the agreement. It is important to note that in this particular form of giving there is no trustee; all of the assets of the charitable organization, not just the assets contributed by the donor, are pledged against the payment of the annual annuity.

2.1.1. The Deferred Gift Annuity

The deferred gift annuity is tailored to meet the needs of the donor who prefers to receive income at a future date but wants to claim a substantial charitable contribution now. The deduction is based on the age the beneficiary will have attained when payments are first received, and the annuity rate will be based on that same age. Higher rates of return and larger charitable contributions are available under deferred annuity plans because the gift is invested by the college and the return on the investment accrues to the donor's benefit during the period before the first payment is made. This plan is of particular interest to persons in high income brackets who are looking forward to retirement sometime within the next twenty years when income will be lower and a lower tax bracket will apply.

2.2. The Pooled Fund Life Income Plan

The pooled fund life income plan involves commingling gifts of many donors. Such pooling enables the College to take advantage of size and diversity in following an investment policy designed to offer both generous income and relative safety. When a gift is received, it is assigned units or shares in the pool based on the fair market value of the gift. Each year, all of the income received from the pooled fund investments must be distributed, prorated periodically to each donor on the basis of the number of his or her units. The rate of return, based on the total income of the pool, is the same for each unit in the fund.

While income amounts are not guaranteed and the investments in the pool may be changed so as to be responsive to different economic conditions, the variations in payments will be far less in both up and down movement than would be true when a relatively small gift is handled as a single investment fund. Inasmuch as the pooled fund is a form of trust, the assets of the College may not be used to fulfill any of its obligations. Indeed, should the institution cease to exist, the trust would continue under supervision and management appointed by the courts. Obviously this plan appeals to the donor whose gift potential is restricted to sums smaller than an amount which can be prudently and effectively invested separately.

2.3. Charitable Remainder Trusts

2.3.1. Unitrust

The unitrust is established as a separate trust with no commingling with other funds. As a result, a flexible management policy can be followed to meet changing conditions and the investment objectives of the donor can be taken into account. Additional gifts may be made to the unitrust from time to time.

Because the value of the assets can be expected to change from year to year, the unitrust payment will vary in amount each year. The amount to be paid is determined by multiplying a percentage (minimum of 5 percent), mutually agreed upon and stated in the trust agreement, by the value of the assets in the trust, revalued each January 1. The amount to be paid each year is known on the first day of that year. Should the annual income exceed the amount to be paid to the beneficiaries, the excess must be added to the trust principal and reinvested for the benefit of the trust.

In making payment from the basic unitrust, the "three-tier concept" calls for the distribution first of all ordinary income and short-term capital gains (both fully taxed) received by the trust. Next, long-term capital gains (40 percent is taxable) are distributed. Finally, tax-exempt income, and if necessary, return of principal (not taxable) are distributed to make up the total annual amount.

It is conceivable that the assets from such a trust could be materially depleted during the lifetime of one or more beneficiaries. In such case, the income each year would be reduced.

Such risk must be explained carefully to potential donors and all possible steps should be taken to be certain that the risk is understood before such gifts are accepted. Once accepted, regular reporting to the donor as to the status of the assets in the trust is absolutely essential.

2.3.2. Net Income Unitrust

A *net income unitrust* is essentially the same as the basic unitrust except that only earned income may be distributed to the donor. A fixed percentage must be stated in the trust agreement which, when multiplied by the value of the assets in the trust, revalued annually, determines the *maximum* payment to be made to the beneficiary. Any income received by the trust other than dividends or interest cannot be distributed but must be added to the principal of the trust. If the available income is not equal to the maximum payment allowable, the deficiency may be carried forward and made up in subsequent years when income is greater than the allowable payment. If there are no such deficiencies, excess income is added to the principal of the trust. Gifts of real estate and tax-exempt bonds may be most efficiently handled under this form of gift.

2.3.3. Annuity Trust

The *annuity trust* offers the assurance of a fixed dollar income. It combines some of the features of both the gift annuity and the basic unitrust. The donor and the charity are free to agree upon the fixed amount to be paid when the agreement is prepared, but once set, it can never be changed. The amount must be at least 5 percent of the fair market value of the assets placed in the trust when it is created. No additional gifts may be made to the trust after its establishment.

The fixed annual payment for the life of the trust is distributed in the same manner as distribution from the basic unitrust—i.e., under the "three-tier concept." In this case *depletion of the trust prior to the death of the last beneficiary is a* possibility and donors should be clearly advised of the risk before this gift is consummated. At the same time, the possibility of increased value of assets under good management is very real so that the sum available to the charity may grow materially between the time of the gift and the maturity of the contract.

2.3.4. Term Certain Annuity Trust

The term *certain annuity trust* provides for payments to the beneficiaries for a specified number of years (not more than twenty) rather than for life. The principal advantage lies in allowing the donor to maximize income tax deductions immediately while providing income for a specified period of time. The plan is particularly advantageous for donors who wish to help young people get started but do not want to provide income support for life. It can also be established to accumulate funds for a small child's college expenses in later years or to cushion the first years of his or her working career after college.

SECTION 3

Engagement Approach

3.1. General Comments

This section presents a detailed review of the approach employed in the Cost/Benefit Analysis. The approach discussions are presented in the following order:

The theory of the Pomona Plan cost/benefit analysis

Costs

Inflation

Mortality

Benefits

Cost/benefit calculations

As a general introductory comment, this engagement involved the application of traditional cost accounting and financial analysis techniques in a technical setting for which there is no generally recognized body of theory. While other researchers have focused on the costs of fund raising and the related benefits of outright gifts, there has been little research in the specific area of deferred giving fund raising programs. To this extent, the approach used in this engagement is that which, in our judgment, is best suited to addressing the objectives set forth. At the same time, we recognize that further research, some of which may be occasioned as a result of this report, may produce other methodologies which are appropriate to the analysis of deferred giving programs.

Further, there are many features of the Pomona Plan which are not generally common to other deferred giving programs.

For example:

Pomona College does not directly solicit deferred gifts from the College "family," including trustees, faculty, students and their parents, and alumni. This policy, which was adopted at the inception of the program in 1946, is very different from the marketing strategies employed by most college and university deferred giving programs.

Pomona College performs the trust administration and investment management functions of the deferred giving program. While some of the more successful other college and university deferred giving programs also perform these functions, many others engage outside assistance to varying degrees.

From these examples, it can be seen that the approach adopted by Pomona College contains certain features which have implications for the cost of the Pomona Plan. The marketing strategy implies a level of cultivation and solicitation costs which may be different at colleges and universities which actively pursue their "family" members. The trust administration and investment management strategy employed by Pomona College also differs from other programs which employ banks and similar financial institutions.

The methodology for analyzing the costs and benefits of deferred giving programs presented in this report is based on the deferred giving programs as they operate at Pomona College. To the extent that other colleges and universities employ other strategies with respect to the promotion and management of their deferred giving programs, the findings of this report with regard to the returns achieved by the Pomona Plan will not be representative of the performance of the deferred giving programs at these other institutions. However, we believe that the methods developed in this study are of general applicability to charitable institutions engaged in seeking financial support through deferred giving fund raising programs.

3.2. The Theory of the Cost/Benefit Analysis of the Pomona Plan

A major task of this engagement has been to develop a methodology for analyzing the costs and related benefits of deferred giving programs. This section presents the principal theoretical bases upon which the approach is founded.

3.2.1. Projected versus Historical Results

Had comprehensive historical records been available, the historical performance of the Pomona Plan would have been the ideal basis for the analysis of costs and benefits. Working with actual data usually produces findings and conclusions which are supported by what actually happened and, therefore, avoids questions about the basis upon which the conclusions are drawn.

Although the Pomona Plan has been in operation for more than thirty years, the historical records of the College, particularly with regard to costs, are not available in sufficient detail to support a cost analysis prior to the early 1970s. For any analysis which is completely historical in nature, this is an insufficient period. Furthermore, the Tax Reform Act of 1969 completely changed the operation of the pooled fund and introduced the Unitrust and the Annuity Trust. As a result, the inclusion of years prior to 1975 may have introduced historical cost and benefit patterns which bear little relevance to present practices and which contribute little to an understanding of the prospective behavior of costs.

The College's records with regard to costs and benefits *are sufficient* in both content and organization to provide for detailed analyses for the years ended June 30, 1975, through 1979. This period is, we believe, sufficient to provide reasonable assumptions about the performance of the Pomona Plan from the standpoint of both costs and benefits.

These assumptions can and have been used to perform a cost/benefit analysis of the Pomona Plan in the form of a projection. Future costs can be projected based on the recent historical performance of costs at the College. Benefits can be projected based on the agreements in force and the terms of these agreements.

Therefore, the findings and conclusions presented in this study are based on the *projected* results of the performance of costs and benefits related to the deferred giving fund raising programs at Pomona College.

3.2.2. Time Period of the Analysis

Depending on the gift acceptance criteria in use, realization of cash flows from a pool of agreements in force at any point in time requires a period of future years.

Attempts to measure the performance of deferred giving programs based on one year's costs and the same year's releases or new agreements signed overlooks the essence of these types of gifts. Costs are incurred today to obtain agreements whose benefits will be realized over a future period of years. Benefits realized today were obtained as a result of cost expenditures which were incurred over a number of prior years.

It is possible to estimate with reasonable assurance the historical costs of obtaining a pool of agreements which are in force today. Similarly, it is possible, based on analysis of the historical behavior of costs, to project the future costs which will be incurred to maintain and service these agreements until they all have been released.

Therefore, the comparison of costs and benefits must be made over a period of years. This is the approach taken in this study. For example, assume that only one agreement were in force. A comparison of the costs and benefits of that agreement basically involves three ingredients:

—the cultivation and solicitation costs incurred to obtain the agreement or outright bequest.

—the costs incurred to maintain and service the agreement as long as it is outstanding.

—the cash inflows realized from the agreement up to and including the time when the agreement is terminated and the corpus is available to the College.

From this oversimplified example, it can readily be seen that conclusions about the economic effectiveness of a deferred giving fund raising program should recognize the timing of the cash flows involved and should, therefore, be based on analyses which encompass these timing issues.

3.2.3. Full Cost

In financial analysis, it is customary to approach decisions about new investments or programs based on the incremental costs which these programs will add to the existing costs. This marginal analysis is the basis of new investment decision making.

On the other hand, a financial analysis of a program which is in place and producing both costs and revenues requires a different approach. To assess the performance of this type of program, one should capture the total costs incurred by the program and compare these costs with the total revenues produced over the time period in question.

In the specific instance of a deferred giving program, costs include not only the actual costs of the specific fund raising department, but also some portion of all of the other departments of the college or university which directly or indirectly support the efforts of the deferred giving program.

With respect to the inclusion of costs which are not directly incurred by the fund raising department (charged with obtaining deferred gifts), such as the Vice President for Development or the President, the involvement of these departments in support of the deferred giving program consumes some portion of the resources these departments have to contribute to the College. If the President were not involved in the deferred giving program, his energies could be directed elsewhere. In this sense, which is generally referred to as opportunity cost, there is a cost related to the support of a deferred giving program provided by every department.

This definition of cost is generally described as full cost—that is, what is the total cost impact of a deferred giving program on the operations of a college or university? This is the definition which has been applied to the cost analysis phases of this engagement.

3.2.4. Variability of Historical Costs

The analysis of historical cost information which was performed during this study demonstrated that the costs of a mature deferred giving program do not vary significantly as a result of changes in new agreements entered into or dollars of agreements in force. While the study period was limited to five years, costs appear to be largely fixed. In view of the very significant amounts of assets under management and the number and dollar value of new agreements signed each year, it is not surprising that the costs of the Pomona Plan demonstrate these patterns.

With specific regard to agreement maintenance costs, it has been assumed that these costs are variable against measures which express the volume of agreements under management. However, the mature deferred giving program experiencing moderate and regular growth in the volume of agreements requiring management is likely to find these costs are fixed over reasonably wide ranges in volume.

3.2.5. Benefits

Accepting the fact that fund raising programs are designed to attract cash *which can be used* in perpetuating the mission of the institution, the definition of benefits produced by a deferred giving program is rather straightforward.

The benefit of a deferred gift is the cash to be realized therefrom. For the purposes of this study, a benefit is clearly not an agreement entered into. The event of signing an agreement produces:
—the realization that the cultivation and solicitation costs incurred in obtaining the gift were invested productively.
—the need to incur annual future costs to maintain and service the agreement during the lives of the donors and/or their beneficiaries.
—the expectation of cash to be received at some future date.

Projections of costs to operate a deferred giving program, given the assumption that the program will continue to exist, are relatively straightforward if a sufficient body of historical data is available. Projections of future agreements to be entered into, on the other hand, are extremely difficult, not withstanding the volume of historical data. From our research, it appears that many factors which are beyond the control of a deferred giving program influence the actual receipt of gifts. Therefore, the expectation that a given level of effort by a deferred giving program will produce a certain level of agreements by number and dollar amount is at conflict with the experience of most deferred giving programs.

Based on the five years of data available in this study with regard to costs and benefits, there was no meaningful relationship between the costs incurred in cultivation and solicitation efforts and agreements signed. While we suppose that such patterns would appear over longer time periods, the five year history does not support any predictable relationship between cultivation and solicitation costs and agreements signed.

Therefore, an analysis of benefits to be received should focus on the existing pool of agreements. This is the approach taken in this study.

Benefits, as defined in this study, include cash flows derived from bequests both as outright gifts and testamentary trusts. While outright bequests are not strictly deferred gifts, they are included in this analysis because of the cultivation and solicitation practices at Pomona College and because of the general acceptance of their inclusion under the term "deferred giving" at most institutions.

With specific regard to outright bequests—those gifts in which the gift amount is immediately available for use by the College—this study treats the benefits in both an historical and projected context. In the historical context, performance is measured by comparing the actual amounts received during the period 1975–1979 with the allocated cultivation and solicitation costs incurred to obtain these amounts. In the projected context, the methodology employed deviates from that employed for other gift categories in that a projection of new gifts has been prepared. The College has a long record of annual outright bequest receipts which is reasonably stable when considered in light of inflation in gift estate values and when viewed in multi-year increments. The overall Pomona Plan internal rate of return which is presented in the findings section of this report includes a projection of annual future outright bequests receipts and cultivation and solicitation costs (table 5.3.4).

3.2.6. Investment Analysis

The cost/benefit analysis of the Pomona Plan involves comparisons of cash flows which occur many years apart. Inflation has a significant influence on the benefits received. A current gift of $100,000 will purchase a $100,000 of goods and services. A deferred gift with a current market value of $100,000 which will be spendable in twenty-five years may, at 6 percent annual inflation, only purchase approximately $23,000 of goods and services in today's dollars, if there is no diminution or increase in the original principal amount over the life of the agreement.

To make financial decisions about programs with these kinds of cash flows, some common definition of the value of a dollar spent or received is essential. This definition is the present value of a dollar— a technique which allows comparison of cash flows in differing time periods by stating these dollars as if they were spent or received in the same period.

The findings of this study with respect to the return on investment of deferred giving programs are based on the application of present value theory to the cash flows produced.

The calculation method applied is the internal rate of return (IRR), which is defined as the interest rate which equates the present value of the expected receipts from agreements in force to the cost of obtaining those receipts.

While the percentage returns which result from the IRR can be expressed in the traditional cost per dollar of gifts received, there are significant differences which should be noted. Most traditional annual and capital giving fund raising programs, as distinct from deferred gift programs, do not require continued management efforts after the gift has been received. The cost per dollar of gift measure is clearly the cost of obtaining the right to receive dollars. It does not address the question of when those dollars will be received— which is the pivotal question in deferred giving. It does not address those situations in which two types of costs are incurred: the cost of obtaining a gift agreement and the cost of managing that agreement during the period of its existence. Therefore, the traditional measurement of costs per dollar of gift received does not address the economic complexities of deferred giving fund raising programs.

For outright bequests, which are not deferred gifts, the historical approach to cost/benefit analysis described in the preceding section does not require the application of the IRR technique. Outright bequests do result from experience in some period of cultivation and solicitation efforts. The receipt of the principal amount of the gift is not contingent upon the lives of certain beneficiaries and is therefore not postponed over some future period.

Therefore, the investment analysis of outright bequests can be entirely historical in nature—that is, no projections of future costs or benefits are required. The most complex aspect of measuring the performance of outright bequests is the identification of the cultivation and solicitation costs incurred to obtain the gift. This is discussed in the following section.

As described in the preceding section on Benefits, this study also treats outright bequests in a projected context. Here, the

IRR calculation does include a projection of future outright bequest receipts based on a review of the history of the program over the period 1975–1979.

3.3. Approach to Costs

This section presents a discussion of the elements involved in defining and projecting the costs of the deferred giving programs at Pomona College. These discussions are supportive of the methodology which is presented in the "Findings" section of this report. The elements are presented in the approximate order in which they have been executed.

3.3.1. Definition of Costs

The preceding section of this report presents the rationale for the definition of costs as the full costs incurred by Pomona College to operate the deferred giving program.

To identify the various departments at Pomona College which contribute costs in support of the deferred giving program, we:
—interviewed the principal officers of the College who are involved in the deferred giving program.
—studied the historical accounting records of the College to identify departments which may be reasonably expected to be involved in supporting the deferred giving program. (The accounting records of the College do not assign costs based on an allocation to the various using departments. Rather, costs are accumulated and reported in the department from which the service originates. This system of accounting classification is by far the most common approach for colleges and universities in the United States.)

Based on this research, we determined that the following departments of the College contribute some cost in support of the Pomona Plan:
Vice President for Development
Annual Giving
College Relations
Office of Public Relations
Publications

Alumni Office
Annuity and Trust
Treasurer's Office
President's Office
Business Office
Auditing
Mail Center
Personnel Administration
Personnel Services
Unemployment Insurance
Business Services
Information Processing
Mimeograph
Utilities
Sumner Hall
Other miscellaneous

The nature of the costs incurred by these departments may be summarized as development, business office support, clerical support, and facilities operation and maintenance.

3.3.2. Cost Findings

Next, we began research to obtain data on the historical costs in total for each of these departments. This involved accumulation of accounting information for the fiscal years 1975–1979 for each department described above. The results of this effort are presented in table 5.1.1.

3.3.3. Identification of Costs Incurred to Support the Deferred Giving Program

The next phase was designed to identify how much of the total cost of each department was related to supporting the deferred giving program.

The Director of Annuity and Trusts (the deferred giving officer), the Vice President for Development, and Treasurer were interviewed to obtain their perceptions regarding the relative level of support and types of costs contributed by each department defined above.

We then conducted detailed interviews with the department head or executive responsible for each identified department. The interviews involved a review with the executive of each expense incurred to develop preliminary assumptions regarding the allocation of costs to the deferred giving program. In most departments, the major expense category was salaries and related employee benefits.

Following these interviews, we conducted, in conjunction with the officers most directly involved in the College's development programs, a review of the preliminary cost allocation summaries to determine their reasonableness. This review produced final allocation strategies which were employed to assign costs from each department to the deferred giving program. The results of these allocations are presented in Table 5.1.2.

While these discussions resulted in the allocation of the same percentage of cost each year within a department, such an approach could be overly simplistic if the total department budget is changed for reasons unrelated to the support of the deferred giving program. While this was generally not the case at Pomona, other institutions should be alert for such changes, which would, if material, necessitate a change in the allocation percentage from year to year.

3.3.4. Division of Costs Within the Deferred Giving Program

At Pomona College, the deferred giving program includes four groups of gift categories:

—gift annuities
—pooled trust funds
—separately managed trusts
—bequests, in the form of outright gifts

Those bequests which create deferred gifts through annuity and trust agreements are included in the gift annuity, pooled fund, and separately managed trust categories.

For each of these gift categories, the College maintains separate records on agreements in force. Further, preliminary research indicated that each of these gift categories experiences differing costs based on the number and dollar value of agreements in force, the marketing efforts to obtain each category of gift, and the varying degrees of difficulty of managing the invested assets and servicing the agreements in force.

Therefore, it was determined to further allocate the costs of the deferred giving program into each of these four gift categories. In addition to the reasons cited above with regard to differing cost levels, it is also true that the investment strategies and, therefore, the benefits to be realized by the various gift categories differ.

In addition to allocating costs between the four gift categories, the cost accounting also had to recognize and consider the functional types of costs incurred in the operation of the deferred giving program.

There are two general categories of costs or functions performed in the deferred giving program. These are:
—cultivation and solicitation costs
—agreement maintenance costs

For the purposes of this study, cultivation and solicitation costs are defined as those costs incurred in initially obtaining an agreement. Any costs relating to an agreement or pool of agreements after they have been obtained and are under management are not considered to be cultivation and solicitation costs.

Agreement maintenance costs are those expenditures which are incurred to manage agreements from the date of the gift to the date of the termination of the annuity or trust agreement.

This segregation of costs into the two functions of cultivation and solicitation and agreement maintenance costs creates a matrix approach to allocating deferred giving program costs. The matrix is graphically presented in table 3.3.4. The reader will note that no agreement maintenance costs have been allocated to outright bequests. For the purposes of this study, it has been assumed that no further costs are incurred on outright bequests after receipt of the gift.

Table 3.3.4. Deferred Giving Costs

Cost Categories	Gift Annuities	Pooled Funds	Separately Managed Trusts	Outright Bequests	Total
Cultivation and solicitation	$xxxx	$xxxx	$xxxx	$xxxx	$xxxx
Agreement maintenance	xxxx	xxxx	xxxx		xxxx
	$XXXX	$XXXX	$XXXX	$XXXX	$XXXX

3.3.5. Allocation of Deferred Giving Costs by Gift Category and Types of Costs

Having completed the identification of departmental costs and having allocated these costs to the deferred giving program in total, the next task involves the determination, in sequential order, of:

—how the costs allocated to the deferred giving program are separated by function between cultivation and solicitation and agreement maintenance.

—how cultivation and solicitation and agreement maintenance costs are divided into the gift categories of gift annuities, pooled funds, separately managed trusts, and outright bequests.

Allocation of costs between cultivation and solicitation and agreement maintenance costs was based 1) on our analysis of the historical experience of the Pomona Plan in terms of new agreements entered into during the fiscal years 1975–1979; 2) on a review of the policies of the deferred giving program during those years in terms of organization, staffing, and management direction; and 3) on the judgment of the deferred giving officer and his associates.

Assumptions were developed about the historical separation of costs and the costs incurred by each department were divided into the two categories. Table 5.1.3 presents a summary of the results of this approach.

An analysis of the history of agreements obtained during the fiscal years 1975–1979 was the basis of allocating cultivation and solicitation costs between gift categories. Table 5.1.4 presents the base data for this analysis.

A separate marketing study of the new agreements established during the fiscal years 1975–1979 determined that the average time between the first expression of interest by a donor and the date of first gift was two years. Assuming an average of twenty-four months, the allocation of costs between gift categories in year 1 depends on the actual gifts obtained both in years 1 and 2. This approach of calculating cultivation and solicitation costs by gift category recognizes the length of time required to obtain agreements and assigns costs based on this recognition.

Only cultivation and solicitation costs have been allocated to outright bequests, on the grounds that no further efforts are required after receipt of the gift.

Agreement maintenance costs, in contrast to cultivation and solicitation costs, do not appear to be heavily influenced by the addition of new agreements to an established pool of gifts. The major factors influencing the behavior of these costs are the number of agreements in force and the relative complexity of managing each type of agreement.

Allocation of maintenance costs between gift categories was based on judgments about the factors described above developed in discussions with the deferred giving officer and his associates. The allocation bases developed are presented in table 5.1.5.

3.3.6. Other Costs Directly Related to the Deferred Giving Program

In addition to the allocated costs for the departments defined in the section entitled "Definition of Costs," several other categories of costs are incurred by the College to support the deferred giving program. These costs include:

—Trust administration fees. These costs are paid to outside investment counselors who assist in managing the assets held in trust.
—Custodial fees. These costs are paid to commercial banks for services related to paying, collecting, and asset safekeeping.
—Real property expenses. The deferred giving program at Pomona College regularly receives both improved and unimproved real property as part or all of the assets that are given to make up an agreement. While it is generally the policy of the College to sell these assets, expenses such as insurance and property taxes may be incurred during the period over which the real properties are held for sale.

Table 5.1.6 presents a detailed summary of the allocation of departmental and other costs by function and gift category.

3.3.7. Estimating Cultivation and Solicitation Costs

The approach to this study focuses on the pool of agreements in force as of June 30, 1978, and the cash flows to be derived from these agreements. With the exception of the projected alternative for treating outright bequests, the analyses do *not* assume that any new agreements will be added after 1978.

Cultivation and solicitation costs are those costs incurred to obtain

new agreements. In this context, several observations are warranted:
—Cultivation and solicitation costs were incurred over the history of the Pomona Plan to obtain the agreements in force at June 30, 1978.
—Developing estimates for the cultivation and solicitation costs incurred to obtain the agreements in force at June 30, 1978, should give recognition to these historical costs, based on fiscal years 1975–1979, *but should not assign additional costs for cultivation and solicitation efforts to be made in the future to attract new agreements.*

An analysis of the historical cultivation and solicitation costs over the fiscal years 1975–1979 makes it possible to estimate the average cost per agreement incurred to obtain the agreements in force at June 30, 1978. The methodology is as follows:
—Determine the average period of time spent cultivating and soliciting new agreements. For the purposes of this projection, it has been assumed that the average period required to obtain a new gift is twenty-four months.
—Restate the five-year historical costs in 1978 dollars by inflating these costs for 1975, 1976, and 1977 and by deflating the 1979 costs.
—Calculate the restated historical cost in 1978 dollars per new agreement obtained during fiscal years 1975–1979. Table 5.1.7 presents the results of these calculations.

Using this approach, cultivation and solicitation costs have been assigned to both outright bequests and annuity and trust agreements.

3.3.8. Projecting Maintenance Costs

Maintenance costs include four categories of historical costs:
—department allocations
—real property expenses
—trust administration fees
—custodial fees

Unlike cultivation and solicitation costs, maintenance costs can be expected to continue throughout the term of each agreement in force.

The approach to projecting maintenance costs has been:
—Department allocations: Historical analysis reveals that these costs vary over time most directly with dollars of agreements under management. The projecting method applied to department al-

locations is based on cost per dollar of agreement under management. As the dollars of agreements under management decline over the projection period, the total departmental allocated maintenance cost declines in constant dollars.

—Real property expenses: These costs are related to ownership of real property received in gift annuities and separately managed trusts. It is the general policy of Pomona College to sell these assets. Therefore, real property expenses have been projected to decline to zero over the relatively brief periods of two years for gift annuities and five years for separately managed trusts. (It should be noted that Pomona's policy with regard to sale of real property may differ from that of other charitable institutions.)

—Trust administration and custodial fees: As with the departmental allocations, historical analysis reveals that these costs vary most directly with dollars under management. The projection of these costs is based on an historical cost per dollar of agreement under management. As the dollars under management decline over the period of the projection, these expenses decline in 1978 dollars.

3.4. Approach to Inflation

The projections of costs and benefits are based in part on future expectations regarding inflation. In general, costs and changes in market yield factors are functionally related to cost inflation. While projections of future price levels are subject to great uncertainty, there is a body of economic theory which supports projections of macroeconomic variables. These theories are the basis for the several macroeconometric models which are used by various well-known banking, business, and educational institutions, including such as the University of Pennsylvania's Wharton Econometric Model, the DRI model, and Chase Econometrics.

To develop projections of the future cost inflation and market yield factors which were necessary to this engagement, we consulted Dr. F. Gerald Adams, Director of the Economics Research Unit at the Wharton School of the University of Pennsylvania. Relying in part on results produced by the Wharton Econometric Model, Dr. Adams provided the projections presented in table 5.2.1 and labeled "Wharton." Three other models were used for the purpose of comparison with the Wharton results. These models were developed by: the University of California at Los Angeles, shortened to "UCLA" in this report; Data Resources, Inc. of Lexington, Massachusetts, abbreviated as "DRI" in subsequent discussions; and the Claremont Economics Institute, referred to as "Claremont." The application of these projections is discussed below.

3.4.1. Annual Rate of Change in the Consumer Price Index

This series describes expected annual increases in general consumer prices and, for the purposes of this study, provides the basis for annual increases in costs as a function of general inflation. While there is some evidence in the literature to suggest that colleges and universities have experienced levels of general cost inflation below the Consumer Price Index in recent years, it did not appear reasonable to assume that this pattern, if real, could continue over a large number of future years.

3.4.2. Interest Rates on High-Grade Corporate Bonds

Significant portions of the investment portfolios of the Pomona Plan are invested in high-grade (investment quality rating AA or better) corporate bonds. This projection of rates has been applied to project changes in bond interest rates at reinvestment dates.

3.4.3. Capital Appreciation in "Blue Chip" Stocks

A smaller but significant portion of the investment portfolios consist of "blue chip" stocks. While the recent performance of the stock markets calls into question any approach which would regularly increase the market values in stocks, that recent experience is not consistent with the long-term performance record. To project long-term appreciation in "blue chip" stocks, the factor for the annual rate of change in the Gross National Product (GNP) deflator has been applied.

3.4.4. Dividend Yield

In addition to capital appreciation on corporate stocks, Pomona College also receives annual cash flows from dividends. To project future dividends, it was necessary to develop assumptions regarding the rate at which dividends would be paid. This factor—the dividend yield—is the cash dividend paid as a percentage of current market price. Dr. Adams provided a working formula for estimating long-term dividend yields, which is:

Dividend yield = Interest rates on high-grade corporate bonds, plus

a factor for risk in the range of 2–3%, minus

a factor for stock capital appreciation, which is the GNP deflator.

It should be understood that even large changes in the dividend yield factors applied in this projection have only limited impact on the findings because of the limited amount of corporate stocks in the Pomona portfolio. Changes in the Pomona policy would impact this observation. Other institutions with different portfolio strategies should develop their own factor for dividend yield.

As described in "Approach to Benefits" (section 3.6), we also analyzed the impact of other econometric models on the findings of this study.

3.5. Projection of Expected Mortality Rates

Inasmuch as virtually all agreements are terminated by death, mortality is an important consideration in the development of projected benefits.

3.5.1. Historical Analysis

We evaluated donor record sheets provided by Pomona College for each of its approximately 750 contributors to the deferred giving program. Because virtually all agreements include more than one life, the mortality analysis was based on approximately 1,500 lives.

A data base was constructed consisting of donor name, age, sex, year of birth, year of death (if applicable), and year of first gift for each donor.

The data base was supplemented with beneficiary data similar to the donor data explained above.

We calculated a mortality rate for each donor and beneficiary. The mortality rate is defined as the number of deaths historically experienced in the Pomona Plan divided by the quantity of lives exposed to the risk of death for a period of one year (referred to as life years of exposure).

One aggregate table was developed based on the combination of combined male and female mortality rates. This table was based on the actual Pomona Plan ratio of male to female donors and beneficiaries. Changes in the ratio of males to females at other institutions could have a significant impact on mortality patterns.

3.5.2. Projected Mortality Rates

Based on the historical analysis described above, the results were compared to annuity tables in current usage within the insurance industry.

The difference between an individual who purchases a life insurance policy to insure against the hazard of dying and a purchaser of an annuity was recognized. Generally speaking, individuals who purchase annuities tend to be in better physical and mental condition than those purchasing life insurance policies. Therefore, annuity tables are more appropriate comparative bases when evaluating annuity programs than tables utilized to compute life insurance policies.

Comparisons were made to two insurance industry tables. The 1977 annuity table and the 1971 Individual Annuity Mortality Table were compared to the Pomona Plan experience.

Adjustments were made to the 1971 Individual Annuity Mortality Table to bring it in line with actual Pomona Plan experience. The adjusted table formed the basis for mortality evaluations in this study (see table 5.2.2).

3.6. Approach to Benefits

In this study a benefit is defined to include the cash proceeds from outright bequests, annuities, and trust remainder interests, and the net cash flows related to annual interest or dividend income less payments related to servicing agreements.

3.6.1. Gift Categories

We reviewed the terms under which each of the major agreement categories operate. This included not only a review of how each agreement category is structured legally but also a review and analysis of payment policies, interest and dividend income expectations, mortality guarantees, and beneficiary limitations.

Pomona Plan agreements fall into three principal categories: gift annuities, pooled income funds, and separately managed trusts. Each type of agreement has unique advantages that make it possible to satisfy specific donor objectives. Pomona College acts as the trustee for the pooled income funds and the separately managed trusts. In that capacity, the College acts as a fiduciary, solely responsible for investment decisions designed to give equal weight to the interests of the income payees and the remainderman. When it is decided to liquidate the assets which are contributed, it is the function of the College's investment advisory firm to select investments which will satisfy both the terms of the agreement and the fiduciary responsibilities of the College.

3.6.1a. Gift Annuity. This agreement amounts to a purchase by the donor of an annuity policy from the College. The difference between the present worth of the annuity policy and the amount contributed by the donor is the charitable gift which qualifies as an itemized deduction for income tax purposes. The annual payment is a fixed dollar amount, which will not vary during the lifetimes of the annuitants. As is the case with commercial annuities, part of the annual payment is considered to be a distribution of earnings, which is taxable as ordinary income in the hands of the annuitant. The other part of the payment is a distribution of principal and is excluded from taxation. Consequently, it is common to invade principal to make the annual payments. The College seeks to have at least 50 percent of the original principal amount remaining at the time the agreement is terminated and the assets in the annuity account are released to the College.

3.6.1b. Pooled Income Fund. This category, established in 1969, is a single investment account within which the contributions of many donors are commingled. This is a unitized pool, meaning that principal and income interests are prorated according to units or shares. The value of one unit varies from month to month, being computed by dividing the market value of the fund's assets by the number of units assigned to payees. When a donor makes a contribution to the fund, a number of units is assigned based on the market value of the contribution and the value of one unit on the contribution date. The number of units assigned to an individual agreement never changes. All dividend and interest income earned in the pooled investment accounts is distributed, an equal amount of income being paid for each unit held by a payee. The College benefits from the release of units at the termination of each pooled fund agreement, i.e., in virtually all cases, the death of a life beneficiary, including the capital appreciation that may have increased the value of each unit.

3.6.1c. Separately Managed Trusts. There are several forms of such trusts, differing principally in how trust income will be distributed to the payees. The investments in each trust may not be commingled with other assets and the College is not permitted to make loans or advances to a trust. In effect, income distributions can be made only from the earnings produced by that trust's assets. If the distribution of ordinary income does not meet the terms of the trust, principal assets of the trust must be sold and the cash proceeds distributed. There are three categories of separately managed trusts:

—Annuity trusts.

—Charitable remainder unitrusts (referred to as Basic Unitrusts by Pomona College).

—Net income (or Income-only) unitrusts. (Pomona College refers to a Net Income Unitrust that is fully invested in municipal bonds as a tax-exempt income trust.)

NOTE: Pomona College still manages a pooled fund and separately managed trusts that were established prior to the 1969 Tax Reform Act. The management of these pre-1969 agreements is governed by different rules and regulations regarding income distributions and investment guidelines. At present, only trust agreements which conform to 1969 Tax Reform Act (the three shown above and the pooled income fund described in the preceding paragraph) can be established if the charitable deductions are to be realized.

Annuity trust. The required annual payment is a fixed dollar amount, which like the payments under a Gift Annuity, will not change during the lifetimes of the payees. If the trust earns more income than needed for the required payment, the excess is treated as if it were capitalized and is reinvested. If the trust earns less income than needed to meet the required payment, the trustee must liquidate principal and distribute the cash proceeds. As is the case with all trusts, if the trust assets should be exhausted (by either investment losses or invasion—or both) before the payees have died, the trust is terminated and no further income payments are made. This would be highly unusual, however, as evidenced by the fact that no trust has ever been terminated before the death of the payees in Pomona College's thirty-five years of experience. When a trust is terminated by the death of the last payee named in the trust instrument, the value of the trust assets that are released to the College will be influenced by the amount of dividend and interest income earned during the term of the trust, by capital appreciation of the trust assets, by distributions from principal, and by the mortality experiences of the last payee to die.

Basic unitrust. The required annual payment is computed by multiplying the market value of the trust assets (as of the first day of the calendar year) by a fixed percentage. Each trust will have its own percentage specified in the trust instrument and that percentage will not change during the lives of the payees. As a consequence, the required payment will fluctuate from year to year as the market value of the trust assets change. As described for the annuity trust, excess income is reinvested and income deficiencies are made up by distributing principal. The same rules affecting termination of annuity trusts apply to unitrusts. The same factors influencing the value of the remainder from annuity trusts when released to the College apply to unitrusts.

Net income unitrust. The required annual payment is either the dividend and interest income received by the trust during the tax year—or a fixed percentage of the value of the assets as revalued each year—whichever is less. Each trust will have its own fixed percentage specified in the trust instrument and that percentage will never change. As in the previous discussion of annuity trusts and basic unitrusts, excess income which cannot be distributed under the terms of the trust will be reinvested as if it were capitalized. In this instance, however, principal is not distributed as part of the annual payment. But, there may be a "make-up" provision which permits the trustee to distribute "excess" income if in any prior trust year the amount of income actually distributed was less than the amount computed by multiplying the fixed percentage by the market value of the assets in that year. The effect of this make-up provision is to insure that no ordinary income will be capitalized if it could have been distributed in an earlier year had it been earned. As in the case of other separately managed trusts, the value of the remainder is determined by the factors already listed, except that depletion of trust assets as a result of invasion will not occur.

Pre-1969 trusts. The required annual payment is simply the amount of the dividend and interest income received by the trust. There are no limits on the amount of income that can be distributed and there is no provision for distributing principal. The asset value at the time of release to the College is influenced by the same factors as the more modern trusts, except again invasion of principal is not permitted.

3.6.2. Mix of Portfolios

We verified the historical cost and fair market value balances and the number of agreements by plan type as of June 30, 1978.

Consideration was given to the investment policies currently being adhered to by the Pomona Plan. We discussed with the College and investment advisers alternate investment strategies.

The resulting approach incorporates a portfolio mix of 80 percent bonds and 20 percent equities, which is the approximate present portfolio composition. It also recognizes that the average bond term in the current investment portfolio of the Pomona Plan is twelve years. Therefore, during the projection period, the portfolio is expected to turnover approximately one and one-half times into bonds carrying different interest rates than those currently being held.

This report also presents the results of return on investment calculations assuming portfolio mixes of 100 percent bonds and 60 percent bonds–40 percent stocks.

3.6.3. Application of Yield Factors

Projected yield factors were required to properly account for bond interest rates, dividend yield factors, and capital appreciation at release date.

Bond interest rates for taxable and tax-exempt bonds were provided by four different econometric models. Tax-exempt bond interest rates were assumed to be 3 percent less than the forecasted yields on taxable bonds. We assumed that bonds currently held in the Pomona Plan portfolio would be retained until their maturity. At maturity date, they would be replaced with bonds carrying new market rates (referred to as "portfolio turnover") or released to the general endowment fund due to donor or beneficiary death.

The factors necessary to calculate dividend yields on stocks were provided by each of four econometric models (Wharton, UCLA, DRI, and Claremont). Dividend yields were incorporated into this approach because 20 percent of the Pomona Plan investment portfolio consists of stocks. These dividends, added to interest earned on bonds, provide the ordinary income accruing to all investments. Dividend yields were forecasted at 2 percent above bond interest rates, less the capital appreciation factor.

When a $10,000 twenty-year bond matures, $10,000 is available. We have assumed that bonds released to the General Endowment Fund due to donor mortality are fully mature. Therefore, no gains or losses on the sale of bonds is recognized. This assumption was the only practical means of approaching bond values at release dates based on the available data.

Stocks are impacted by gains and losses. Capital appreciation on stocks which have been released due to mortality and sold at market rates in excess of their historical book value, have been accounted for in this forecast. Capital appreciation was projected based on annual increases in the GNP deflator.

The GNP deflator is the most comprehensive price index in the United States. Bond rates, dividend yields, and capital appreciation are all assumed to be in some fashion linked with the GNP deflator.

Each of the econometric models utilized in this study produced factors which were used in developing assumptions about yield factors.

The following economic models were utilized in the calculation of benefits:

Base Case—Wharton
Expected Case—Wharton
Alternative Expected Cases—UCLA, DRI, Claremont
Portfolio Mix Change Case—Wharton

It is important in the application of yield factors to the projection of benefits that internal consistency be maintained. Therefore, we did not feel it to be suitable to utilize one econometric model for bond interest rates, another for dividend yield factors, and a third for capital appreciation of stocks. We retained internal consistency by presenting cases based exclusively on assumptions prepared by one particular econometric model.

3.6.4. Outright Bequests

We obtained historical data on the number and dollar value of gifts received as outright bequests each year during the fiscal years 1975–1979. This data allowed a direct calculation of returns by comparison with allocated cultivation and solicitation costs based on the historical approach described elsewhere in this report. For the IRR calculations, a projection of future annual receipts has been prepared based on data on annual receipts for the period 1975–1979. The projection of annual receipts and the historical data upon which it is based are presented in table 5.3.4.

3.6.5. Cases to be Presented

We developed seven projected benefit cases to illustrate the range and sensitivity of the results. These cases do not include outright bequests.

3.6.5a. *Base Case.* The base case is designed to answer the question: What would the results be if current bond interest rates and current stock prices did not change during the projection period? The base case presents a situation which is unrealistic in fact but useful for purposes of contrast with the other alternatives presented.

3.6.5b. Expected Case. The expected case utilizes the Wharton forecast of yield factors (bond interest, dividend yield factors, capital appreciation) applied to an 80 percent bonds–20 percent stocks portfolio. This mix approximates the actual current structure of the portfolios. Although the portfolio mix does not change during the projection period, the College has been assumed to reinvest the proceeds of maturing bonds into similar quality bonds. Releases at fair market value are estimated according to the mortality projection developed for this study and the projection of capital appreciation.

3.6.5c. Alternative Expected Cases. Three alternative cases are also presented. Each assumes the same portfolio mix as the Expected Case. The only difference is that yield factors were developed by UCLA, DRI, and Claremont. Portfolio turnover assumptions are also the same as in the Expected Case.

3.6.5d. Portfolio Mix Change Case. Currently, the portfolio mix of the Pomona Plan consists of approximately 80 percent bonds and 20 percent stocks. To illustrate the sensitivity of the Pomona Plan securities portfolio yield to changes in portfolio mix, we also prepared two more cases. The Wharton yield factors (bond interest, dividend income, and capital appreciation) were utilized in the preparation of a 60 percent bonds, 40 percent stocks case and a 100 percent bonds, 0 percent stocks case. Other assumptions such as portfolio turnover and capital appreciation on released securities remained the same.

In summary:

	Alternative Cases Presented				
Portfolio			Alternative		
Mix	Base	Expected			
(bonds)	(Wharton)	(Wharton)	(UCLA)	(DRI)	(Claremont)
100%		X			
80%	X	X	X	X	X
60%		X			

3.6.6. Method of Projecting Releases

Based on an analysis of all contracts in force as of June 30, 1978, and of all contracts which were released prior to that date, we developed a specific mortality table for the donors to the Pomona Plan. The analysis focused on each contract and gave specific consideration to the age of the donor where relevant, i.e., where the donor is the payee, and all identified beneficiaries.

We projected releases based on aggregate mortality percentages by year. It is inconsistent with the theory of mortality to predict a particular year when a particular donor would be expected to die. Therefore, our approach applies the same mortality release percentages to each fund's beginning balance on an annual basis. The effect on this approach is to project releases based on annual fractional deaths applied to the entire gift portfolio.

For each contract in force, we identified the stated payout rates and the basis on which these rates are calculated. In general, these contracts specify fixed payments in certain dollar amounts or variable payments based on investment yields for each year in which an agreement remains outstanding. The yield realized in cash from the investments related to each agreement provides the source of payment of the stated payout rate. If this income should not satisfy the terms of a trust agreement, some of the principal must be liquidated to make the payments. Annual cash yields include dividend streams from equities and interest payments from bonds.

We assumed that equities are held until the release date of the contract and that bonds are reinvested in securities of similar investment qualities when they mature. We gave consideration to the impact of higher or lower interest rates on bonds at the projected reinvestment dates.

For agreements with fixed payout conditions, we proceeded on the understanding that shortages of cash from investment yields are made up from the principal amount of the agreement and that annual cash excesses over the fixed payment amount remain in the fund and result in an increase in the principal amount available for investment. The exception is gift annuities. It is our understanding that excesses or shortages of cash from investment yields are offset against mortality releases to the General Endowment Fund.

For agreements in which shortages of cash yields available to meet fixed payment agreements result in the total consumption of the principal available from the agreement, we have assumed that—with the exception of gift annuities—no further payments are made once principal is exhausted. Under gift annuities, the College is required to continue making payments from general College assets.

Payouts were determined by the particular agreement in question.

Income depends on the assumed portfolio mix, a reinvestment assumption, and the alternate rate of return projections of interest income on bonds and dividend yield projections for equities.

The value of an agreement at release date is impacted by capital appreciation and fair market value factors to adjust the portfolio's historical basis to projected fair market value. Bonds which are released are assumed to be fully mature. The projected yields were provided by the four principal econometric models.

3.7. Approach to Internal Rate of Return Calculations

The results of this study with respect to the costs and benefits of the Pomona Plan, excluding outright bequests, are expressed as the internal rate of return on a series of cash flows which have the following three components:

Solicitation and cultivation costs;

Agreement maintenance costs;

Benefits.

The major steps are as follows:

Table 5.1.7 presents the total historical cultivation and solicitation cost in 1978 dollars for all of the agreements in force at June 30, 1978. These amounts are treated as cash outflows in 1978—that is, the total historical cost to obtain all of the agreements in force by gift category in 1978 dollars.

Agreement maintenance costs are projected as annual cash outflows in current (inflated) dollars in each year of the projection period. As described above, these amounts have been allocated between gift categories. In general, maintenance costs decline annually over the projection, before the application of inflation, as a function of declining asset balances under management.

Table 5.3.1 presents the projected annual cash inflows resulting from the releases of agreements in force at June 30, 1978.

These three series (cultivation and solicitation costs, agreement maintenance costs, and benefits) were then summarized into a single stream of net cash flows over a period of twenty future years (through 1998). Our analysis indicates that the present value of cash inflows after twenty years, assuming that releases would continue over some future number of years, has a minimal impact on calculated internal rates of return.

Internal rate of return calculations were performed on each of the seven benefit alternatives under consideration. For the historical approach to outright bequests, the calculations involved an annual comparison of gifts received with allocated cultivation and solicitation costs. The historical returns presented for outright bequests, expressed as cents of cost per dollar of benefit received, represent the average of the five year returns for the fiscal years 1975–1979 (Table 5.3.3).

Finally, a total program IRR was calculated by combining the expected cases for each annuity or trust category with projected annual receipts, net of projected cultivation and solicitation costs, for outright bequests.

SECTION 4

Engagement Findings

The findings which follow are divided into two groupings which relate to the major tasks of this study:

1. A methodology for analyzing the costs and benefits of deferred giving programs, including annuities, trusts, and bequests.
2. The specific results of the execution of this methodology at Pomona College.

4.1. Methodology

The approach section of this report presents detailed information about the methods employed. This Findings section presents a review of the methods employed, in the expectation that other charitable institutions may seek to apply the methods to their programs.

The steps which follow are presented sequentially. The work on historical costs can generally proceed at the same time as that related to mortality and benefits.

Step 1. *Define costs to be included in the analysis.*
  A. By interview and examination of the financial statements of the institution, determine which departments support (contribute services to) the deferred giving program. The nature of the costs incurred may be summarized as *development, business office support, clerical support, and facilities operation, and maintenance.*
  B. Identify "outside" costs such as trust administration, investment advisors, and real property expenses which are incurred in support of the program.

Step 2. *Gather Historical Cost.* Gather historical data on the total costs of these departments or "outside" costs for a period of three to five years. If available, five years of data are preferable. The most recently completed fiscal year makes a convenient ending point for this analysis.

Step 3. *Determine the portion of total annual cost for each department or "outside" cost which is attributable to support of the deferred giving program.*

A. Assuming that the accounting records do not directly provide this information, first interview the executives most directly involved in the deferred giving program.

B. Conduct similar interviews with the department heads or outside contractors to obtain their impressions.

C. Develop the apportionment based on these findings. The portion of each department's cost allocated to the deferred giving program may vary each year or may be constant as a percentage of total cost.

Step 4. *Divide the resulting total deferred giving costs by type of cost and gift category, if relevant.*

A. We defined costs as either cultivation and solicitation or agreement maintenance costs. The gift categories applied were gift annuities, pooled funds, separately managed trusts, and outright bequests.

   1. We suggest dividing total costs first into types of cost (cultivation and solicitation and agreement maintenance) and then into the various gift categories.

   2. These divisions should avoid excessive detail. Too many categories of costs or gifts requires judgments about the behavior of historical costs which are excessively detailed and highly judgmental.

   3. Certain types of costs, such as publications or special events, are not clearly distinguished as either cultivation and solicitation or agreement maintenance costs. There are no definitive guides to support the allocation of these types of costs. The allocations should be reasonable and should be applied consistently.

B. The division of costs into cultivation and solicitation or agreement maintenance was based chiefly on a review of the policies of the deferred giving program during the fiscal years 1975–1979 with regard to organization, staffing, and management direction and on discussions with the deferred giving officer and his associates. These discussions focused on the nature of the support provided to the deferred giving program by each department identified in step 3 above. In the absence of more definitive historical information, this approach was selected as the easiest and most likely to produce dependable results.

This analysis should also consider the "outside" costs discussed in step 1, which are likely to be mainly agreement maintenance costs.

Step 5. *Gather projections of inflation and market yield factors.* The indices used should be those which, in the judgment of the executives of the deferred giving program, are most appropriate to the specific circumstances. Most charitable institutions will need the following indices:

A. A cost inflation index.
B. Interest rates in high grade corporate bonds.
C. Capital appreciation in investment quality stocks. If the investment portfolio does not include corporate stocks, this information will not be necessary.
D. Dividend yields. While the formula used in this study may be useful, each institution may wish to select its own approach.

Step 6. *Decide on a mortality projection which best describes the donors and beneficiaries of the deferred giving program.*

A. The table presented in this study has been tailored to the Pomona College experience based on more than 1,500 lives. Because of its comprehensiveness, it is very well suited for analyses of this nature.
B. Some actuarial advice in the selection of an appropriate table may be desirable.

Step 7. *Develop basic data about agreements in force.*

A. We suggest that agreements in force be as of the last day of the most recent year included in the cost analysis.
B. As of the date used to determine agreements in force, the basic data should include:
   1. type of gift.
   2. age of donor and beneficiaries.
   3. terms of payment associated with the gift.
   4. market value of the gift assets.
   5. value of gift at time of signing of agreement.
   6. types of assets under management.
C. Based on the data gathered above and on the defined mortality table, we recommend converting each agreement into

one equivalent life to simplify the projection of releases. This involves the combination of male and female results, defined as "years of exposure" (or one life living one year) into one aggregate table based on their occurrence in the actual population of the plan. For instance, in the case of the Pomona Plan, 43.5 percent of the donors and beneficiaries of the Plan are male, 56.5 percent are female. The aggregate years of exposure for males and females were combined based on the actual male/female ratio of the Plan. The resulting aggregate table was then compared to industry tables commonly in use. The Pomona College aggregated one-life table compared favorably to the Society of Actuaries' 1971 individual annuity mortality table, adjusted for a 10 percent decrease in mortality.

Step 8. *Project annual cash inflows, payments, and releases from agreements in force.*

A. The projection consists of several key components. They are:
1. the annual payment terms of each agreement.
2. the market yield factors described above.
3. the equivalent one life for each agreement.

B. Based on this data, projections of annual cash flows and releases can be prepared either by agreement, by gift category, or in total for the entire program. The decision as to which level should be used depends chiefly on the size and complexity of agreements in force. This step has the following components:
1. Annual cash flows are the cash receipts produced from interest or dividend payments compared to the stated payout requirements of the agreements. These cash flows may decrease, increase, or have no impact on the remaining principal value of each agreement in force.
2. Release dates should be based on mortality tables. We suggest projecting releases based on the probabilities contained in the mortality tables and *not* as a single point.
3. The amount of cash available at release depends on a) the impact of annual cash flows in increasing or decreasing the original value of an agreement, and b) the market values of the stocks and bonds at the date of release. The market values can be projected using the market indices developed in step 5 above.

C. Remember that this methodology does not include consideration of the prospective impact of new agreements to be signed. It focuses only on agreements in force.

Step 9. *Determine historical cultivation and solicitation costs.*

A. Because these costs are defined to have been included in connection with the signing of agreements, there will be no projection of future cultivation and solicitation costs.

B. Using the historical data developed in step 4, determine the total historical cultivation and solicitation cost per agreement in force. This determination requires:

1. Evaluating the average period of time required in obtaining a gift.

2. The number of new agreements entered into in each year of the historical analysis period.

3. Conversion of historical costs to equivalent dollars. We suggest inflating costs incurred before the most recent year of the cost data into that year's dollars.

C. Based on the agreements signed during the historical period under analysis, evaluate the historical cultivation and solicitation costs per new agreement signed. Apply this cost amount to the total number of agreements in force.

D. These methods will result in total current dollar estimates of cultivation and solicitation costs by gift category. This is the data required for the IRR analysis.

Step 10. *Develop projection methods for historical agreement maintenance costs.*

A. These costs will continue as long as there are agreements to service in force.

B. We suggest projecting future agreement maintenance costs based on the recent cost per dollar of agreements in force. (In the case of Pomona College, the cost amount was stated in 1978 dollars.) The calculated cost amount is multiplied by the dollars of agreements in force each year.

C. This method allows maintenance costs to decline in constant dollars as the volume of agreements declines over the future years.

D. Future agreement maintenance costs should also be inflated annually by the application of the cost inflation index developed above.

Step 11. *Combine the projections of agreement net annual cash inflows, releases, cultivation and solicitation costs, and future agreement maintenance costs and perform the IRR analysis*

A. The cash flow stream which is the basis of the IRR calculation consists of the following elements:

1. The estimated cultivation and solicitation costs, which are treated as a cash outflow in the beginning period.
2. The estimated net annual cash inflows and releases from agreements in force.
3. The estimated future annual agreement maintenance costs for each year in which cash flows are projected.

B. Based on the execution of this workplan at Pomona College, we recommend limiting the forecast period for benefits and agreement maintenance costs to not more than twenty years. Our analysis indicates that cash inflows occurring after the twentieth year have relatively little impact on the findings from this methodology.

Step 12. *Outright bequests.* Step 4 produced an allocation of cultivation and solicitation costs to outright bequests for each year of the historical period. Compare these annual costs with the annual dollar volume of gifts and compute a five-year average of cents per dollar of benefits received. This cost figure may be converted to an average percentage return for the historical period by the formula:

$$\text{Average \% Return} = \frac{1 - \text{Average Cents Per Dollar}}{\text{Average Cents Per Dollar}}$$

Because these percentages are likely to be extremely high, it may be more meaningful to simply describe the return as cents of cost per dollar of benefit achieved.

For the purposes of the IRR calculations which combine gift annuities, pooled funds, separately managed trusts, and outright bequests, it is necessary to project annual receipts from outright bequests. We suggest that this projection be based on all available historical information on annual receipts and give explicit consideration to increases in annual receipts during the projection period because of the impact of inflation on increasing the value of gift estates. Projections of annual receipts should be reduced by projections of the cultivation and solicitation costs related to obtaining outright bequests.

This section of the report has presented a review of the methodology produced as one of the major tasks of this assignment. This report now continues to address the findings resulting from the specific application of this methodology to the Pomona Plan.

4.2. Cost

The various appendixes present a detailed review of our findings with respect to cost. During our work, we have observed that:

Most costs of a deferred giving program such as that in place at Pomona College are relatively fixed in nature and, therefore, should not be expected to vary significantly over time for an established program.

The most prominent exception to this statement relates to salaries and related benefits costs in the deferred giving office itself. These costs are highly subject to control by College administration.

The most significant costs incurred historically are the deferred giving department and the business office. At Pomona, these costs account for approximately 85% of the total department costs allocated to the deferred giving program.

4.3. Mortality

The mortality section of this study yielded the following findings as they relate to the donors of the Pomona Plan.

The Pomona Plan's mortality experience correlates very closely to the 1971 Individual Annuity Mortality Table, adjusted for a 10 percent decrease in mortality. The adjustment is necessary because donors to the Plan are living slightly longer than the table predicts and, with expected improvement in medical science, are expected to continue experiencing some improvement in mortality over what the 1971 IAM Table would indicate.

Over twenty years, 84 percent of the principal held in annuities are expected to have been released to Pomona College; 56 percent and 52 percent of all monies held in pooled income and separately managed trusts, respectively, are projected to have been released. This reflects the appeal of gift annuities to relatively older donors.

4.4. Benefits

The annual cash flows to be realized under the expected case alternative are presented in table 5.3.1. It should be noted that the cash inflows from agreements in force at June 30, 1978, do not vary materially between varying sets of market yield and cost inflation assumptions.

We investigated the possible impact of large donations on the results of this study, were the beneficiaries to die earlier than expected. Our finding is that donors contributing in excess of $300,000 each have frequently identified more than one beneficiary. This implies that it will most likely take a long period of years to cause the release of a majority of the largest agreements.

The internal rate of return will be favorably impacted by releases in advance of the timing projected in this study.

4.5. IRR

Table 4.5.1 presents the findings resulting from calculations of the internal rate of return under each identified alternative. For outright bequests, the history of the program for the period 1975–1979 indicates an average cost per dollar of benefit received of approximately 2.2¢. The historical details for outright bequests are presented in table 5.3.3.

Table 4.5.1 illustrates that the internal rates of return produced by the various gift categories are:

—all positive, which is to answer the basic question, "Do we make any money as a result of the deferred giving program?" Pomona College does receive net positive cash inflows from the Pomona Plan.

—very attractive when measured against other investment yields available in the general economy.

To convert these IRR factors to the traditional evaluation of costs per dollar of benefits received, the calculation is to divide $1.00 by the percentage return expressed as 1 plus the percentage. For example, for gift annuities under the Wharton Expected Case, the calculation is (1/1.519), yielding the answer that this alternative requires approximately 66¢ to obtain one dollar of benefits. As we point out in section 3.2.6, the application of this traditional fund raising measure to deferred giv-

Table 4.5.1. Internal Rates of Return: the Pomona Plan

| | Assuming No Change in Existing Portfolio Mix (80% Bonds–20% Stocks) | | | | | Wharton Expected Case Assuming a Bond Portfolio Mix of | |
| | | Wharton Expected Case | Alternate Cases | | | | |
	Base Case		DRI	UCLA	Claremont	60%	100%
Gift annuities	45.4%	51.9%	61.8%	64.2%	45.8%	48.0%	56.5%
Pooled funds	23.5%	27.7%	26.9%	26.6%	25.9%	29.5%	25.8%
Separately managed trusts	13.2%	18.4%	17.8%	14.8%	15.8%	18.6%	18.4%

Table 4.5.2. Costs per Dollar of Benefits Received: the Pomona Plan

| | Assuming No Change in Existing Portfolio Mix (80% Bonds–20% Stocks) | | | | | Wharton Expected Case Assuming a Bond Portfolio Mix of | |
| | | Wharton Expected Case | Alternate Cases | | | | |
	Base Case		DRI	UCLA	Claremont	60%	100%
Gift annuities	.69	.66	.62	.61	.69	.68	.64
Pooled funds	.81	.78	.79	.79	.79	.77	.79
Separately managed trusts	.88	.84	.85	.87	.86	.84	.84

ing programs presents serious conceptual issues and, in our judgment, fails to address the economic complexities of deferred giving fund raising programs.

A review of the results of the IRR calculations illustrates the relative sensitivity of the findings to the assumptions about future inflation rates and changes in market yields. This observation is consistent with the beliefs of many deferred giving officers and argues strongly for agreement forms which minimize a charitable institution's exposure to future changes in these factors.

Based on the approach applied in this study, it is also possible to make certain observations about the cultivation and solicitation cost experience of the Pomona Plan. Based on data for the five years in question, the cultivation and solicitation cost per dollar of agreements in force (that is, excluding outright bequests) as of June 30, 1978, is 8.7¢.

This answer—8.7¢ per dollar of agreement—is specifically the "cost" of establishing the agreements from which future benefits will be received. The answer is not theoretically different from the standard cost per dollar of benefits received in measuring the "effectiveness" of annual giving programs. In the instance of deferred giving programs, the standard question might be rephrased "what is the cost of obtaining the right to receive dollars in the future in the form of agreements signed today?"

The calculated IRR for the Pomona Plan in total, based on the expected case and including gift annuities, pooled funds, separately managed trusts, and projected receipts from outright bequests is 92 percent. Clearly the addition of outright bequests, which are relatively low cost in comparison to other gift categories, improves the returns calculated. By traditional investment standards, the returns achieved by the Pomona Plan are extremely attractive.

Each college and university engaged in deferred giving will have gift categories, acceptance criteria, and investment policies which differ from the position of the Pomona Plan. For this reason, the total return produced by the deferred giving programs at each institution is likely to vary from that achieved by the Pomona Plan.

SECTION 5

Data Summaries

5.1. Cost Data

Table 5.1.1. Historical Costs of Departments Contributing Costs to the Deferred Giving Program
(dollars in thousands)

	For the Years Ending June 30,				
	1975	1976	1977	1978	1979
Vice President for Development	$ 64	$ 71	$ 97	$ 93	$ 84
Annual Giving	63	68	62	66	80
College Relations				67	74
Office of Public Relations	14	30	31	71	88
Publications	54	57	54	52	
Alumni Office	150	162	113	118	175
Annuity and Trust	160	196	161	195	205
Treasurer's Office	48	49	69	81	76
President's Office	105	110	114	221	136
Business Office	185	219	249	265	225
Auditing	13	18	25	24	82
Mail Center		9	18	18	21
Personnel Administration	14	19	20	30	38
Personnel Services	25	29	22	25	33
Unemployment Insurance	11	9	47	30	25
Business Services	37	32	12	12	14
Information Processing	60	54	61	67	80
Mimeograph	40	43	16	11	10
Utilities	6	70	58	11	9
Sumner Hall	22			42	58
Other miscellaneous	67	159	298	112	156
TOTAL	$1,138	$1,404	$1,527	$1,611	$1,669

Table 5.1.2. Department Costs Allocated to the Deferred Giving Program
(dollars in thousands)

	For the Years Ending June 30,				
	1975	1976	1977	1978	1979
Vice President for Development	$ 11	$ 11	$ 11	$ 13	$ 14
Annual Giving				3	2
College Relations				.2	.2
Office of Public Relations				1	4
Publications	2	3	2	2	
Alumni Office	.3	.5	.1	.1	.1
Annuity and Trust	157	194	159	192	199
Treasurer's Office	2	2	3	3	3
President's Office	2	2	3	3	3
Business Office	28	34	38	41	69
Auditing	2	3	4	4	7
Mail Center	1	1	1	1	1
Personnel Administration	.1	.2	.2	.3	.4
Personnel Services	.3	.3	.2	.3	.3
Unemployment Insurance	.1	.1	.5	.3	.2
Business Services	.2	.2	.1	.1	.1
Information Processing	6	5	6	7	8
Mimeograph	.5	.8	.3	.3	.3
Utilities		.3	.3		
Sumner Hall	1			2	2
Other miscellaneous	.1	.4	.7	.1	.1
TOTAL	$213.6	$257.8	$299.4	$273.7	$313.7

Table 5.1.3. Allocation of Deferred Giving Costs
(dollars in thousands)

	For the Years Ending June 30,				
	1975	1976	1977	1978	1979
Solicitation and cultivation	$131.5	$157.7	$134.3	$166.5	$173.3
Agreement maintenance	82.1	100.1	95.1	107.2	140.4
TOTAL	$213.6	$257.8	$299.4	$273.7	$313.7

NOTE: In table 5.1.6, these costs are described as "Department Allocation."

Table 5.1.4. New Agreements by Gift Category

| | | For the Years Ending June 30, | | | |
		1975	1976	1977	1978	1979
Gift annuities		15	14	20	21	12
Pooled funds		15	12	11	9	13
Separately managed trusts		21	29	35	43	60
Outright bequests		26	26	28	25	38
	TOTAL	77	81	94	98	123

Table 5.1.5. Percentage Allocation of Agreement Maintenance Costs by Gift Category

	Percent of Total Agreement Maintenance Cost
Gift annuities	5
Pooled funds:	
pre–1969	5
post–1969	5
Separately managed trusts	
Tax exempt	5
Unitrusts	60
Annuity trust	20
	100

Table 5.1.6. Deferred Giving Program Cost Allocation Matrix
(dollars in thousands)

Gift Category	Cost Type	For the Years Ending June 30,				
		1975	1976	1977	1978	1979
Gift annuities	Department allocation[a]	$ 29/4	$ 32/5	$ 24/5	$ 22/5	$ 17/7
	Real property expenses	/8	/6	/12	/7	/2
	SUBTOTAL	29/12	32/11	24/17	22/12	17/9
Pooled funds	Department allocation[a]	23/8	19/10	14/9	17/11	18/14
	Trust administration fees	/19	/17	/20	/19	/17
	Custodial fees	/10	/11	/11	/11	/8
	SUBTOTAL	23/37	19/38	14/40	17/41	18/39
Separately managed trusts	Department allocation[a]	53/68	61/81	59/78	79/87	85/115
	Trust administration fees	/11	/10	/12	/14	/17
	Custodial fees					/6
	Real property expenses	/17	/17	/31	/29	/15
	SUBTOTAL	53/96	61/108	59/121	79/130	85/153
Outright bequests	Department allocation[a]	26/3	46/3	37/3	48/3	53/4
	TOTAL[b]	$131/148	$158/160	$134/181	$166/186	$173/205

NOTE: % Numbers are presented as: Cultivation and Solicitation/Agreement Maintenance.
[a] The "Department Allocation" represents those costs presented in table 5.1.3.
[b] Totals may not agree to prior schedules due to rounding. Agreement maintenance costs include Trust Administration Fees, Custodial Fees, and Real Property Expenses.

Table 5.1.7. Historical Cultivation and Solicitation Cost per Agreements
(1978 dollars)

	Agreements in Force June 30, 1978	Historical Cost per Agreement (1978 $)	Total Historical Cost by Gift Category
Gift annuities	213	$1,679	$ 357,627
Pooled funds	1,190	$1,656	$1,970,640
Separately managed trusts	405	$1,903	$ 770,715

NOTE: Table 5.3.3. presents data on outright bequests.

5.2. Reference Data

Table 5.2.1. Economic Predictions, June 30, 1978

| | Wharton | | | UCLA | | | DRI | | | Claremont | | |
| | General inflation | GNP deflator | AAA bond market yield | General inflation | GNP deflator | AAA bond market yield | General inflation | GNP deflator | AAA bond market yield | General inflation | GNP deflator | AAA bond market yield |
Year												
1	11.7%	9.1%	9.9%	10.9%	8.9%	9.3%	10.9%	8.9%	9.5%		8.4%	9.4%
2	11.8	9.3	9.8	9.5	7.8	9.2	9.6	8.6	9.0		10.7	10.1
3	8.9	7.6	9.4	7.1	6.8	8.6	8.6	8.7	9.4		8.4	10.0
4	7.4	7.7	9.7	6.7	6.6	8.2	8.2	8.2	9.7		3.9	9.1
5	6.6	6.8	9.3	6.5	6.5	8.0	7.5	7.7	9.8		2.1	6.7
6	6.7	6.7	9.0	6.4	6.6	7.8	7.4	7.6	9.8		2.3	5.1
7	6.3	6.4	8.9	6.2	6.7	7.7	7.4	7.4	9.7		3.6	5.7
8	6.5	6.4	8.7	6.1	6.6	7.6	7.1	6.9	9.6		6.1	6.8
9	6.2	6.1	8.6	6.0	6.2	7.5	6.9	6.6	9.5		7.9	8.5
10	5.9	5.8	8.4	5.9	6.0	7.4	6.9	6.6	9.3		8.6	9.9
11	5.6	5.6	8.4	5.8	6.0	7.4	6.8	6.5	9.2		8.8	10.3
12	5.5	5.4	8.4	5.7	5.9	7.3	6.7	6.4	9.1		8.9	10.5
13	5.6	5.6	8.4	5.7	5.9	7.3	6.7	6.4	9.1		8.9	10.5
14	5.6	5.6	8.4	5.7	5.9	7.3	6.7	6.4	9.1		8.9	10.5
15	5.6	5.6	8.4	5.7	5.9	7.3	6.7	6.4	9.1		8.9	10.5
16	5.5	5.5	8.1	5.7	5.9	7.3	6.7	6.4	9.1		8.9	10.5
17	5.5	5.5	8.0	5.7	5.9	7.3	6.7	6.4	9.1		8.9	10.5
18	5.4	5.4	8.0	5.7	5.9	7.3	6.7	6.4	9.1		8.9	10.5
19	5.2	5.3	8.0	5.7	5.9	7.3	6.7	6.4	9.1		8.9	10.5
20	5.3	5.3	8.0	5.7	5.9	7.3	6.7	6.4	9.1		8.9	10.5

Table 5.2.2. 1971 Individual Annuity Mortality Table Adjusted by 10 Percent Mortality Improvement Factor

			Yearly Death Rate Per 1,000				
Age	Male	Female	Combined[a]	Age	Male	Female	Combined[a]
40	1.47	.85	1.12	73	30.42	17.77	23.27
41	1.61	.91	1.21	74	33.28	20.03	25.79
42	1.80	.98	1.34	75	36.44	22.61	28.63
43	2.03	1.07	1.49	76	39.95	25.53	31.80
44	2.31	1.16	1.66	77	43.85	28.83	35.36
45	2.63	1.26	1.86	78	48.15	32.61	39.37
46	2.99	1.37	2.07	79	52.91	36.88	43.85
47	3.38	1.49	2.31	80	58.14	41.75	48.88
48	3.81	1.62	2.57	81	63.81	47.26	54.46
49	4.27	1.77	2.86	82	69.90	53.47	60.62
50	4.76	1.94	3.17	83	76.45	60.44	67.40
51	5.27	2.13	3.50	84	83.58	68.31	74.95
52	5.81	2.38	3.87	85	91.52	77.19	83.42
53	6.38	2.67	4.28	86	100.49	87.21	92.99
54	6.97	3.02	4.74	87	110.75	98.41	103.78
55	7.58	3.41	5.22	88	122.51	110.68	115.83
56	8.21	3.85	5.75	89	135.96	123.76	129.07
57	8.87	4.35	6.32	90	151.24	137.22	143.32
58	9.55	4.87	6.91	91	168.44	150.63	158.38
59	10.27	5.42	7.53	92	187.61	163.60	174.04
60	11.03	5.97	8.17	93	208.70	175.85	190.14
61	11.82	6.50	8.81	94	231.44	187.26	206.48
62	12.66	6.99	9.46	95	255.46	197.91	222.94
63	13.57	7.46	10.12	96	280.41	207.99	239.49
64	14.57	7.90	10.80	97	306.19	217.99	256.36
65	15.66	8.36	11.54	98	332.79	228.44	273.83
66	16.89	8.90	12.38	99	360.17	239.81	292.17
67	18.26	9.56	13.34	100	388.27	252.49	311.55
68	19.79	10.39	14.48	101	416.98	266.81	332.13
69	21.50	11.39	15.79	102	446.18	283.09	354.03
70	23.40	12.63	17.31	103	475.74	301.61	377.36
71	25.51	14.09	19.06	104	505.52	322.69	402.22
72	27.84	15.80	21.04	105	535.39	346.61	428.73

NOTE: IAM Table reduced by 10 percent.

[a] Combination effected in accordance with actual Pomona Plan experience (43.5 percent males, 56.5 percent females).

Table 5.2.3. Summary of Agreements in Force as of June 30, 1978

Fund	Number of Agreements in Force	Dollar Value (at historical cost)
Gift annuities	213	$ 5,521,000
Pooled income	1,190	18,328,000
Separately managed trusts	405	11,783,000
TOTAL	1,808	$35,632,000

SOURCE: Number of agreements in force and the dollar value of those agreements as of June 30, 1978, were developed from individual donor record sheets provided by Pomona College for each donor to the Pomona Plan.

5.3. Benefit Data

Table 5.3.1. Expected Case Releases for Gift Annuities, Pooled Funds, and Separately Managed Trusts
(dollars in thousands)

Year	Gift Annuities	Pooled Funds	Separately Managed Trusts	Total Releases from the Expected Case
1	$ 146	$ 522	$ 192	$ 860
2	254	533	199	986
3	200	548	212	960
4	225	570	232	1,027
5	252	596	257	1,105
6	279	716	281	1,276
7	307	651	299	1,257
8	326	677	318	1,321
9	342	699	334	1,375
10	347	761	346	1,454
11	354	773	357	1,484
12	357	779	362	1,498
13	355	780	364	1,499
14	349	774	365	1,488
15	342	763	357	1,462
16	327	749	342	1,418
17	310	731	333	1,374
18	291	712	323	1,326
19	270	691	309	1,270
20	248	669	291	1,208
Balance remaining at the end of the twentieth year	$1,466	$12,698	$11,102	$25,266

NOTE: This table presents the 80 percent bond portfolio assumption. The releases are stated at the amounts expected to be realized based on projected fair market values.

Table 5.3.2. Expected Case Releases—Five-Year Intervals

Millions of Dollars	5 yrs.	10 yrs.	15 yrs.	20 yrs.
$7.50			* 7.44	
7.25				
7.00				
6.75		* 6.68		* 6.60
6.50				
6.25				
6.00				
5.75				
5.50				
5.25				
5.00	* 4.94			
4.75				
4.50				
4.25				
4.00			○ 3.87	
3.75				
3.50		○ 3.50		○ 3.55
3.25				
3.00				
2.75	○ 2.77			
2.50				
2.25				
2.00			× 1.81	
1.75		• 1.60	• 1.76	× 1.60
1.50	× 1.09	× 1.58		• 1.45
1.25				
1.00	• 1.08			
.75				
.50				

• Gift annuities
○ Pooled funds
× Separately managed trusts
* Total

Table 5.3.3 Outright Bequests

	Number of Gifts	Allocated Cultivation and Solicitation Costs	Dollars of Gifts Received
1975	26	$25,300	$1,883,700
1976	26	46,000	873,600
1977	28	37,700	2,646,800
1978	25	48,800	1,222,900
1979	38	53,368	2,980,800

SOURCE: College records.

Table 5.3.4 Projecting Outright Bequests

Actual Historical Receipts		Projected Annual Receipts	
Year	Amount	Year	Amount
1965	$1,084,000	1980	$1,950,000
1966	1,453,000	1981	2,070,000
1967	359,000	1982	2,190,000
1968	255,000	1983	2,310,000
1969	545,000	1984	2,432,000
1970	364,000	1985	2,553,000
1971	1,512,000	1986	2,675,000
1972	482,000	1987	2,795,000
1973	969,000	1988	2,916,000
1974	1,376,000	1989	3,037,000
1975	1,884,000	1990	3,158,000
1976	874,000	1991	3,278,000
1977	2,647,000	1992	3,399,000
1978	1,123,000	1993	3,520,000
1979	2,981,000	1994	3,641,000
		1995	3,762,000
		1996	3,883,000
		1997	4,004,000
		1998	4,125,000

NOTE: The projection is based on a trend line of three-year moving averages for the period 1965–1979.

SECTION 6

Cost/Benefit Analysis Work Sheets and Reference Tables

6.1. Cost/Benefit Analysis Work Sheets

This section contains cost/benefit analysis work sheets for annuity, charitable trust, and bequest programs for colleges and universities. The simplified approach represented in these work sheets was developed from the study performed by E&W on the Pomona Plan of Pomona College, Claremont, California. They represent a simplified approach to a complex set of issues. Although the work sheets may or may not parallel each characteristic of every program type and contractual arrangement, they can be reasonably expected to bear some resemblance to the key attributes of annuity and trust programs at colleges and universities.

Ernst & Whinney prepared a report describing the background approach, scope, and results of the cost/benefit study performed on Pomona College's Pomona Plan. The report to which these work sheets are appended should be read in its entirety so that the reader may better grasp the complexity of the issues involved and how they were resolved in a manner more theoretically correct than that represented in the simplified work sheets. The work can be grouped generally into two categories of major steps: cost considerations and contract activity considerations.

6.1.1. *Cost Considerations*

1. Determine costs incurred to obtain contracts currently in force.

2. Assess past and projected expected future maintenance costs for the program, including the effect of inflation.

6.1.2. Contract Activity Considerations

1. Determine mortality experience and future mortality expectations.
2. Analyze the contractual features of each agreement type and the manner in which these features are reflected and recorded in the accounting system.
3. Establish the interrelationship between the contract activity and the investment results.
4. Determine the approach towards estimating and projecting donor payouts, mortality releases, and investment results. This would include the following interdependent factors:
   —contracts with multiple donors and/or beneficiaries;
   —payout restrictions that modify the basic payout rule;
   —ability of invested assets to produce income in excess of payout requirements and treatment of deficiencies;
   —market value of future released assets;
   —means of estimating future investment results through measurement of inflation, portfolio mix, current and projected portfolio yields, portfolio turnover, and the corresponding effect of mortality.
5. Reconciliation of past investment portfolio experience and portfolio volume with projected contractual values and releases to determine the reasonableness of results.

A computerized model was developed based exclusively on the historical analysis and projected portfolio attributes of the Pomona Plan. Although the financial model has widespread applicability to established deferred giving programs, it would require adaptation to give adequate recognition to the unique attributes of each college or university's contractual agreements and portfolio objectives.

In an effort to simplify the approach, work sheets were developed that appear likely to produce results comparable to that developed by the financial model. Several important attributes form the basis of these work sheets.

6.1.3. Assumptions

1. Results depend on the reasonable determination and allocation of cultivation, solicitation, and maintenance costs.
2. The work sheets are based on the Pomona Plan and their circumstances and experiences. The resultant assumptions and techniques may not be applicable to other institutions, especially with regard to:
   —types of contracts and contractual obligations;
   —mortality experience;
   —investment experiences and expectations;
   —treatment of investment deficiencies;
   —significance of multiple life contracts.
3. Accuracy of the simplified technique is not assured as the homogeneity of the data may vary with regard to:
   —distribution of single and multiple life contracts;
   —distribution of ages;
   —distribution of dollars among ages and contract types;
   —contractual payout arrangements and restrictions.
4. The technique utilized in the simplified approach is based on broad averages which may vary the ability to reasonably reflect the actual distribution of data in the population.

The work sheets have not been thoroughly tested for each program type nor have the expected results been compared to the results developed when utilizing the financial model. We believe the work sheets represent a reasonable first approximation of cost/benefit internal rates of return.

6.1.4. Benefits

There are, we believe, significant benefits to be derived by colleges and universities in evaluating their current deferred giving program.

1. A study such as this can help determine the value of the program to the institution in terms of dollars expended per benefits received.
2. Projections of releases to the General Fund performed with

the aid of an independently arrived and documented financial model may help manage more effectively the cash flow of the institution and aid in obtaining higher lines of credit from financial establishments.

3. The process of gathering data may provide insight into possible cost efficiencies and improvements in record-keeping techniques.

4. The results should provide an understanding of the volume of the benefits received through a deferred giving program and the factors most seriously impacting its successful outcome.

5. The methodology employed by E&W clearly allows for the development of donor acceptance criteria reflecting the more salient parameters of a deferred giving program.

6. The process also will aid in structuring and designing effective deferred giving contracts.

7. This analysis tends to produce a more acute awareness for which programs provide the greatest potential pay-off to the college and why.

8. It creates an ability to compare each institution's performance with others and improve where necessary.

9. A prospective evaluation can help colleges without any significant deferred giving programs establish a program.

10. Evaluation of cost/benefits of deferred giving programs may uncover strong monetary incentives to expand programs of this nature.

6.1.5. Work sheets 1–15 follow.

The worksheets originally submitted as part of the Ernst and Whinney report have been modified in some cases by the authors to change the format of the worksheets without altering the procedural content that was developed by Ernst and Whinney analysts.

ERNST & WHINNEY
COST/BENEFIT ANALYSIS WORKSHEETS
ANNUITY, CHARITABLE TRUST AND BEQUEST PROGRAM
AS OF JUNE 30, 19___

#1 ANNUITY AND TRUST HISTORICAL COSTS (Any recent five year historical period may be selected as long as consistency
    is maintained throughout the schedules)

Year	1979	1978	1977	1976	1975
Department	A&T Dollars	A&T Dollars	A&T Dollars	A&T Dollars	A&T Dollars
List departments or outside agencies that contribute services to the deferred giving programs net of management fees collected	$	$	$	$	$
Total A&T Dollars	$	$	$	$	$

NOTE: "A&T Dollars" are estimated for each year for each department as follows: Total Expenditures by the department
       multiplied by a percentage estimated to be the portion of the departmental effort applied in that year to
       support of the deferred giving program. Any management fee collected by the department must be deducted before
       entering the net amount.

ERNST & WHINNEY
COST/BENEFIT ANALYSIS WORKSHEETS
ANNUITY, CHARITABLE TRUST AND BEQUEST PROGRAM
AS OF JUNE 30, 19____

#2   ALLOCATED COSTS
      CULTIVATION AND SOLICITATION/MAINTENANCE

(A) Year	(B) Total A&T Dollars	(C) Cultivation %		(D) & Solicitation $	(E) Maintenance %	(F) $	Total %
(Example Years)	W/S #1	Estimate		(BxC)	Estimate	(BxE)	100%
1979							
1978							
1977							
1976							
1975							

162

ERNST & WHINNEY
COST/BENEFIT ANALYSIS WORKSHEETS
ANNUITY, CHARITABLE TRUST AND BEQUEST PROGRAM
AS OF JUNE 30, 19___

#3 ALLOCATED CULTIVATION AND SOLICITATION
    TO GIFT TYPE

(A) Year	(B) C&S Dollars W/S #2 Col D	(C) Gift Annuities % Estimate	(D) $ (BxC)	(E) Pooled Income % Estimate	(F) $ (BxE)	(G) Annuity Trusts % Estimate	(H) $ (BxG)	(I) Unitrusts % Estimate	(J) $ (BxI)	(K) Outright Bequests % Estimate	(L) $ (BxK)
(Example Years)											
1979											
1978											
1977											
1976											
1975											

NOTE: Amount in Column B must equal sum of amounts in Columns D, F, H, J and L.

163

ERNST & WHINNEY
COST/BENEFIT ANALYSIS WORKSHEETS
ANNUITY, CHARITABLE TRUST AND BEQUEST PROGRAM
AS OF JUNE 30, 19___

#4 HISTORICAL C&S COSTS BY
TYPE OF AGREEMENT

	(A)	(B)	(C)	(D)	(E)	(F)
(Check one)	Year	Number of New Agreements	Allocated C&S Costs	Inflation Factor	Cost In 1979 Dollars	Number of Agreements In Force
	(Example Years)	From historical records	W/S #3 Col D, F, H or J	Reference Table 6.2.1	(CxD)	Same as W/S #7 Col A or W/S #8 Col A
___ Gift Annuities	1979					
___ Pooled Income	1978					
___ Annuity Trusts	1977					
___ Unitrusts	1976					
	1975					
Total for 5 years		═══			$═══	═══

Cost Computation: C&S Cost per New Agreement = Five-Year Total in Column E ÷ Five-Year Total in Column B

Historical C&S Costs (1979 Dollars) = C&S Cost per New Agreement x Five-Year Total in Column F = $_____

Note: A separate presentation of data should be prepared for any group of agreements which differs in administrative concept or investment objectives. For example, each of several Pooled Income Funds at the same institution might be analyzed separately.

Inflation factors (Column D) can be obtained from any number of econometric forecasters to update for all subsequent years.

164

#5 ALLOCATED MAINTENANCE COSTS TO GIFT TYPE

(A) Year	(B) Maintenance Dollars W/S #2 Col F	(C) Gift Annuities % Estimate	(D) $ (BxC)	(E) Pooled Income % Estimate	(F) $ (BxE)	(G) Annuity Trusts % Estimate	(H) $ (BxG)	(I) Unitrusts % Estimate	(J) $ (BxI)
(Example Years)									
1979									
1978									
1977									
1976									
1975									

NOTE: Amount in Column B must equal sum of amounts in Columns D, F, H, and J.

165

#6 PROJECTED MAINTENANCE COSTS

(A) Year	(B) Total Dollars Under Management	(C) Total Costs	(D) Cost Per Dollar Under Management	(E) Future Years	(F) Projected Cost Per Dollar Under Management	(G) Projected Dollars Under Management	(H) Projected Annual Maintenance Costs
(Example Years)	Historical records	W/S #5 Col D, F, H or J	Col C ÷ Col B		Best estimate which corresponds to values in Col D. Adjust for projected inflation rate (Reference Table 6.2.1)	Use Beginning of Year Balance from worksheet #10 or #11 as appropriate	(FxG)
1979				1			
1978				2			
1977				3			
1976				4			
1975				5			
				6			
				7			
				8			
				9			
				10			
				11			
				12			
				13			
				14			
				15			
				16			
				17			
				18			
				19			
				20			

(Check one)

_____ Gift Annuities
_____ Pooled Income
_____ Annuity Trusts
_____ Unitrusts

ERNST & WHINNEY
COST/BENEFIT ANALYSIS WORKSHEETS
ANNUITY, CHARITABLE TRUST AND BEQUEST PROGRAM
AS OF JUNE 30, 19___

#7   DONOR DATA

	(A)	(B)	(C)	(D)	(E)	(F)	(G)	(H)
		Agreement Information		Payout		Donor and Beneficiary Information		
	Unique Number	Date	Amount (Dollars)	%	Dollars	Date of Birth	Attained Age	Gift Dollars Weighted by Age
(Check one)								
___ Gift Annuities	Assign a unique number, prefer-ably sequen-tial, to each agreement	Record the date agreement was signed	Note the original gift value	Agreed payout percen-tage (if avail-able)	State every agreed payout in dollars at Year 0	For each payee	Age (to the nearest birthday) on date this calculation is made	(CxG)
___ Annuity Trusts								
___ Unitrusts								
Totals			$ ___		$ ___			$ ___

Computation of Factors: Number of Lives per Agreement = Total Number of Payees (Column F) ÷ Total Number of Agreements (Column A) = ___ .

Weighted Average Payout Rate = (Total Amount in Column E ÷ Total Amount in Column C) X 100 = ___ %.

Weighted Average Age = Total in Column H ÷ Total in Column C = ___ years.

Note: In Column A, several agreements may be lumped together as one agreement if they became effective in the same tax year and included identical terms and payees - or if the new agreements were simply additions to trusts already in existence from prior tax years.

#8   DONOR DATA

	(A) Agreement Information	(B)	(C)	(F) Donor and Beneficiary Information	(G)	(H)
	Unique Number	Date	Amount (Dollars)	Date of Birth	Attained Age	Gift Dollars Weighted by Age
Pooled Income	Assign a unique number, preferably sequential, to each agreement	Record the date agreement was signed	Note the original gift value	For each payee	Age (to the nearest birthday) on date this calculation is made	(CxG)
Totals			$ _____			$ _____

Computation of Factors:

Number of Lives per Agreement = Total Number of Payees (Column F) ÷ Total Number of Agreements (Column A) = _____ .

Weighted Average Age = Total in Column H ÷ Total in Column C = _____ years.

ERNST & WHINNEY
COST/BENEFIT ANALYSIS WORKSHEETS
ANNUITY, CHARITABLE TRUST AND BEQUEST PROGRAM
AS OF JUNE 30, 19___

#9 BOOK VALUE (The market value of each asset in an agreement at the time the asset was acquired by purchase or as a gift)

(Check one)	(A) Year	(B) Beginning of Year Balance	(C) Rate	(D) Payout (Dollars)	(E) Mortality Release Factor	(F) Value Released Dollars	(G) Investment Income Rate (%)	(H) Investment Income (Dollars)	(I) End of Year Balance
Gift Annuities	Year 1: fiscal year in which this calculation is being made	Year 1: obtain from records Years 2-20: Carry forward from Col I	Weighted Average Payout Rate W/S #7	(BxC)	Select factors from Reference Table 6.2.2 most closely associated with the Number of Lives per Agreement on W/S #7 and Weighted Average Age on W/S #7	(BxE)	See Table 6.2.3	(BxG)	(B−D−F+H)
___ Annuity Trusts									
___ Unitrusts (including pre-1969 trusts, tax-exempt income trusts, basic-fixed %, and net income or income-only unitrusts)									
		$ _____	%	$		$	%	$ $	$
	1								
	2								
	3								
	4								
	5								
	6								
	7								
	8								
	9								
	10								
	11								
	12								
	13								
	14								
	15								
	16								
	17								
	18								
	19								
	20								

ERNST & WHINNEY
COST/BENEFIT ANALYSIS WORKSHEETS
ANNUITY, CHARITABLE TRUST AND BEQUEST PROGRAM
AS OF JUNE 30, 19___

#10   FAIR MARKET VALUE (Market value of each asset in an agreement as of the date six months after the beginning of the current fiscal year)

(Check one)
___ Gift Annuities
___ Annuity Trusts

(A) Year	(B) Beginning of Year Balance	(C) Book Value Released	(D) Book Value To Fair Market Value Ratio	(E) Fair Market Value Factor	(F) Releases at Fair Market Value	(G) End of Year Balance
Year 1: fiscal year 1980 (Example Years)	Year 1: obtain from records Years 2-20: Carry forward from Col G	Use values in W/S #9 Col F	Divide value in Col B by value in W/S #9 Col B for the same year	Reference Table 6.2.4 adjusted to end of the fiscal year	(CxDxE)	(BxE) - (F) - W/S #9 Col D + W/S #9 Col H
	$ _____	$			$	$
1						
2						
3						
4						
5						
6						
7						
8						
9						
10						
11						
12						
13						
14						
15						
16						
17						
18						
19						
20						

ERNST & WHINNEY
COST/BENEFIT ANALYSIS WORKSHEETS
ANNUITY, CHARITABLE TRUST AND BEQUEST PROGRAM
AS OF JUNE 30, 19____

#11   FAIR MARKET VALUE (Market value of each asset in an agreement as of the date six months after the beginning of the current fiscal year)

(A) Year	(B) Beginning of Year Balance	(C) Mortality Release Factor	(D) Fair Market Value Factor	(E) Releases at Fair Market Value	(F) End of Year Balance
				(BxCxD)	(BxD) − (E)
Year 1: fiscal year 1980 (Example Years)	Year 1: obtain from records Years 2-20: Carry forward from Col F	Select factors from Reference Table 6.2.2 most closely associated with the Number of Lives per Agreement on W/S #7 or #8 (as appropriate) and Weighted Average Age on W/S #7 or #8	See table 6.2.4		

Pooled Income
Unitrusts

1
2
3
4
5
6
7
8
9
10
11
12
13
14
15
16
17
18
19
20

$ _____ $ $

171

ERNST & WHINNEY
COST/BENEFIT ANALYSIS WORKSHEETS
ANNUITY, CHARITABLE TRUST AND BEQUEST PROGRAM
AS OF JUNE 30, 19____

#12 TOTAL PROJECTED BENEFITS

(A)	(B)	(C)	(D)	(E)	(F)	(G)	(H)
	GIFT ANNUITIES		RELEASES AT FAIR MARKET VALUE		TRUSTS AND POOLED INCOME FUNDS		
		Investment	Releases				
Year	Payout	Income	At Fair Market Value	TOTAL	Pooled Income	Annuity Trusts	Unitrusts
	W/S #9 Col D	W/S #9 Col H	W/S #10 Col F	(C+D-B)	W/S #11 Col E	W/S #10 Col F	W/S #11 Col E
	($	$	$	$	$	$	$
1							
2							
3							
4							
5							
6							
7							
8							
9							
10							
11							
12							
13							
14							
15							
16							
17							
18							
19							
20							

172

#13   CALCULATION OF INTERNAL RATE OF RETURN

Internal rate of return (IRR) is an interest rate that equates the present value of a set of cash flows with an initial investment. It is the interest rate that is obtained when the calculated net present value of a series of cash flows is zero. IRR is also called the yield or discounted rate of return. IRR has been programmed into many hand-held calculators. The method for computing IRR and the accompanying Present Value Tables are found in standard financial management texts such as Managerial Finance, Weston & Brigham, Holt, Rinehart and Winston, 1981.

(Check one)

_____ Gift Annuities
_____ Pooled Income
_____ Annuity Trusts
_____ Unitrusts

Year (A)	Historical Cultivation and Solicitation Costs (B) W/S #4	Projected Annual Agreement Maintenance Costs (C) W/S #6 Col H	Projected Benefits (D) W/S #12 Col E, F, G or H	Annual Cash Flow Stream (E)
0	($_____)			Year 0 = all C&S costs Years 1-20 = (D-C) ($_____)
1				$____
2				$____
3				
4				
5				
6				
7				
8				
9				
10				
11				
12				
13				
14				
15				
16				
17				
18				
19				
20		$____	$____	
		$____	$____	

To perform IRR: Utilize (E) and assume remaining balance will be received evenly over years 21-30.

Remaining Balance $_____

ERNST & WHINNEY
COST/BENEFIT ANALYSIS WORKSHEETS
ANNUITY, CHARITABLE TRUST AND BEQUEST PROGRAM
AS OF JUNE 30, 19___

#14 PROJECTED OUTRIGHT BEQUESTS

(A) Year	(B) Projected Average Annual Bequests	(C) Projected Annual C&S Costs	(D) Net Annual Cash Flows
	Estimated	Estimated based on historical data on W/S #3 Col L	(B-C)
1			
2			
3			
4			
5			
6			
7			
8			
9			
10			
11			
12			
13			
14			
15			
16			
17			
18			
19			
20			

174

#15   CALCULATION OF OVERALL IRR

(A)	(B)	(C)	(D)	(E)	(F)	(G)
			ANNUAL CASH FLOW STREAMS			
Year	Gift Annuities	Pooled Income	Annuity Trusts	Unitrusts	Outright Bequests	Total Annual Cash Flow Stream
	W/S #13 Col E	W/S #13 Col E	W/S #13 Col E	W/S #13 Col E	W/S #14 Col D	
0	($)	($)	($)	($)		($)
1	$	$	$	$	$	$
2						
3						
4						
5						
6						
7						
8						
9						
10						
11						
12						
13						
14						
15						
16						
17						
18						
19						
20						

Remaining Balance $_____

To Perform IRR: Utilize (G) and assume
remaining balance will be received evenly
over years 21-30.

6.2. Reference Tables

Table 6.2.1 Pomona College Projection of Inflation (Wharton Projection)

1975	7.0%
1976	7.0
1977	8.0
1978	8.0
1979	11.7
1980	11.8
1981	8.9
1982	7.4
1983	6.6
1984	6.7
1985	6.3
1986	6.5
1987	6.2
1988	5.9
1989	5.6
1990	5.5
1991	5.6
1992	5.6
1993	5.6
1994	5.5
1995	5.5
1996	5.4
1997	5.2
1998	5.3
1999	5.3

Table 6.2.2 Pomona College Mortality Release Factors

Duration	Age 67			Age 72			Age 77		
	1.1 per Contract[a]	1.3 per Contract[a]	1.5 per Contract[a]	1.1 per Contract[a]	1.3 per Contract[a]	1.5 per Contract[a]	1.1 per Contract[a]	1.3 per Contract[a]	1.5 per Contract[a]
0	0	0	0	0	0	0	0	0	0
1	2.770	1.574	0.916	3.187	1.838	1.082	3.735	2.195	1.313
2	3.342	2.382	1.708	3.853	2.782	2.017	4.517	3.319	2.442
3	3.720	2.891	2.262	4.297	3.381	2.672	5.043	4.032	3.231
4	4.063	3.324	2.739	4.702	3.892	3.238	5.522	4.640	3.912
5	4.394	3.723	3.176	5.095	4.365	3.758	5.985	5.202	4.537
6	4.724	4.104	3.590	5.486	4.819	4.253	6.446	5.740	5.130
7	5.058	4.480	3.992	5.884	5.266	4.734	6.909	6.267	5.704
8	5.401	4.855	4.389	6.292	5.714	5.211	7.381	6.791	6.268
9	5.758	5.238	4.789	6.714	6.170	5.691	7.864	7.319	6.830
10	6.131	5.632	5.196	7.155	6.638	6.179	8.362	7.854	7.396
11	6.525	6.042	5.618	7.617	7.124	6.683	8.877	8.402	7.971
12	6.943	6.474	6.059	8.104	7.632	7.207	9.410	8.964	8.557
13	7.388	6.931	6.523	8.620	8.167	7.755	9.963	9.544	9.159
14	7.864	7.418	7.016	9.168	8.732	8.333	10.536	10.141	9.777
15	8.375	7.939	7.534	9.749	9.331	8.945	11.131	10.758	10.412
16	8.924	8.498	8.108	10.368	9.966	9.593	11.748	11.395	11.067
17	9.514	9.099	8.716	11.026	10.640	10.280	12.388	12.053	11.741
18	10.151	9.746	9.370	11.725	11.355	11.008	13.051	12.733	12.436
19	10.838	10.444	10.076	12.465	12.111	11.778	13.739	13.437	13.154
20	11.577	11.196	10.837	13.246	12.909	12.591	14.454	14.168	13.897

NOTE: This table is based on the actual experience of the Pomona Plan.
[a] Percent of prior year principal.

Table 6.2.3 Pomona College Summary of Rate of Return Factors—Bonds (June 30, 1978)

Year	Wharton Projections			
	Gift Annuities	Pooled Funds	Trusts	Tax-Exempt Trusts
1	6.30	7.65	7.50	5.80
2	6.30	7.65	7.50	5.80
3	6.30	7.65	7.50	5.80
4	6.30	7.65	7.50	5.80
5	6.30	7.65	7.50	5.80
6	6.57	7.79	7.65	5.82
7	6.83	7.91	7.79	5.83
8	7.07	8.01	7.91	5.82
9	7.30	8.11	8.02	5.80
10	7.51	8.21	8.11	5.76
11	7.72	8.26	8.20	5.72
12	7.93	8.34	8.29	5.68
13	8.14	8.41	8.38	5.64
14	8.33	8.46	8.45	5.58
15	8.52	8.52	8.52	5.52
16	8.46	8.47	8.46	5.48
17	8.40	8.42	8.40	5.41
18	8.35	8.37	8.35	5.37
19	8.30	8.32	8.30	5.32
20	8.25	8.27	8.25	5.27

NOTE: This table is based on the data collected for the Pomona Plan. These projections should be adjusted to reflect the portfolio of any given annuity and trust program. These numbers reflect a 100 percent bond portfolio.

Table 6.2.4 Pomona College Summary of Fair Market Value Factors—Bonds (June 30, 1978)

Year	Gift Annuities	Pooled Funds	Trusts	Tax-Exempt Trusts
		Wharton Projections		
1	1.007	1.000	1.007	1.007
2	1.007	1.006	1.008	1.011
3	1.022	1.006	1.017	1.017
4	1.033	1.016	1.024	1.021
5	1.042	1.024	1.031	1.024
6	1.043	1.030	1.032	1.017
7	1.042	1.031	1.031	1.010
8	1.037	1.030	1.026	1.004
9	1.028	1.025	1.015	1.000
10	1.015	1.013	1.006	.997
11	1.013	1.003	1.006	.996
12	1.011	1.003	1.005	.997
13	1.008	1.003	1.004	1.000
14	1.006	1.003	1.003	1.002
15	1.003	1.003	1.003	1.005
16	1.001	1.002	1.003	1.005
17	.999	1.000	.999	1.004
18	.998	.998	.998	1.001
19	.997	.996	.997	.998
20	.997	.993	.997	.996

NOTE: This table is based on the data collected for the Pomona Plan. These projections should be adjusted to reflect the portfolio mix of any given annuity and trust program. These numbers reflect a 100 percent bond portfolio.

APPENDIX B

Internal Rate of Return Calculations: Work Sheets for Wellesley and Grinnell Colleges

APPENDIX 2
INTERNAL RATE OF RETURN CALCULATIONS

WELLESLEY COLLEGE

WORKSHEETS

# 1	Only college-wide annual totals were submitted.
# 2	Historical costs for only three years were submitted.
# 3	No Bequests or Annuity Trusts were reported.
# 4	A detailed analysis of only Gift Annuities is shown.
# 5	Historical costs for only three years were submitted.
# 6	Gift Annuities only.
# 7	Gift Annuities only.
# 8	Omitted.
# 9	Gift Annuities only.
#10	Gift Annuities only.
#11	Omitted.
#12	Gift Annuities only.
#13	Gift Annuities only. Remaining Balance omitted.
#14	Omitted.
#15	Supporting calculations for Pooled Fund and Unitrust have not been included.

Original worksheet formats were used and do not include modifications shown in Section 6.1.5.

ERNST & WHINNEY
COST/BENEFIT ANALYSIS WORKSHEETS
ANNUITY, CHARITABLE TRUST AND BEQUEST PROGRAM
AS OF JUNE 30, 19___

Wellesley College

#1 ANNUITY AND TRUST HISTORICAL COSTS (Any recent five year historical period may be selected as long as consistency
    is maintained throughout the schedules)

Year	1979	1978	1977	1976	1975
Department	A&T Dollars	A&T Dollars	A&T Dollars	A&T Dollars	A&T Dollars
List departments or outside agencies that contribute services to the deferred giving programs net of management fees collected	$	$	$	$	$
			No departmental breakdown provided.		
Total A&T Dollars	$ _____	$101,000	$86,500	$82,700	$ _____

NOTE: "A&T Dollars" are estimated for each year for each department as follows: Total Expenditures by the department
       multiplied by a percentage estimated to be the portion of the departmental effort applied in that year to
       support of the deferred giving program. Any management fee collected by the department must be deducted before
       entering the net amount.

184

ERNST & WHINNEY
COST/BENEFIT ANALYSIS WORKSHEETS
ANNUITY, CHARITABLE TRUST AND BEQUEST PROGRAM
AS OF JUNE 30, 19___

Wellesley College

#2   ALLOCATED COSTS
CULTIVATION AND SOLICITATION/MAINTENANCE

(A) Year	(B) Total A&T Dollars W/S #1	(C) Cultivation & Solicitation % Estimate	(D) Solicitation $ (BxC)	(E) Maintenance % Estimate	(F) $ (BxE)	Total % 100%
(Example Years)						
~~1979~~						
1978	$101,000	54%	$54,900	46%	$46,100	
1977	$86,500	59%	$51,300	41%	$35,200	
1976	$82,700	57%	$47,200	43%	$35,500	
~~1975~~						

ERNST & WHINNEY
COST/BENEFIT ANALYSIS WORKSHEETS
ANNUITY, CHARITABLE TRUST AND BEQUEST PROGRAM
AS OF JUNE 30, 19___

Wellesley College

#3 ALLOCATED CULTIVATION AND SOLICITATION
    TO GIFT TYPE

Year	(B) C&S Dollars W/S #2 Col D	(C) Gift Annuities % Estimate	(D) $ (BxC)	(E) Pooled Income % Estimate	(F) $ (BxE)	(G) Annuity Trusts % Estimate	(H) $ (BxG)	(I) Unitrusts % Estimate	(J) $ (BxI)	(K) Outright Bequests % Estimate	(L) $ (BxK)
(Example Years)											
~~1979~~											
1978	$54,900	44%	$24,484	51%	$27,872			5%	$2,534		
1977	$51,300	58%	$29,787	40%	$20,686			2%	$827		
1976	$47,200	41%	$19,496	57%	$26,678			2%	$1,026		
~~1975~~											

NOTE: Amount in Column B must equal sum of amounts in Columns D, F, H, J and L.

ERNST & WHINNEY
COST/BENEFIT ANALYSIS WORKSHEETS
ANNUITY, CHARITABLE TRUST AND BEQUEST PROGRAM
AS OF JUNE 30, 19___

Wellesley College

#4 HISTORICAL C&S COSTS BY TYPE OF AGREEMENT

(Check one)

___✓___ Gift Annuities
_____ Pooled Income
_____ Annuity Trusts
_____ Unitrusts

	(A) Year	(B) Number of New Agreements	(C) Allocated C&S Costs	(D) Inflation Factor	(E) Cost In 1979 Dollars	(F) Number of Agreements In Force
	(Example Years)	From historical records	W/S #3 Col D, F, H or J	Reference Table 6.2.1	(CxD)	Same as W/S #7 Col A or W/S #8 Col A
	~~1979~~					
	1978	29	$24,494	1.0	$24,494	
	1977	37	29,787	1.07	$31,872	
	1976	18	19,496	1.14	$22,321	
	~~1975~~					
Total for 5 years		84*			$78,687	84*

* Includes Two Deferred Gift Annuities for which no payments are being made at present.

Cost Computation: C&S Cost per New Agreement = Five-Year Total in Column E ÷ Five-Year Total in Column B $ 936.75

Historical C&S Costs (1979 Dollars) = C&S Cost per New Agreement x Five-Year Total in Column F = $78,687

Note: A separate presentation of data should be prepared for any group of agreements which differs in administrative concept or investment objectives. For example, each of several Pooled Income Funds at the same institution might be analyzed separately.

Inflation factors (Column D) can be obtained from any number of econometric forecasters to update for all subsequent years.

ERNST & WHINNEY
COST/BENEFIT ANALYSIS WORKSHEETS
ANNUITY, CHARITABLE TRUST AND BEQUEST PROGRAM
AS OF JUNE 30, 19___

Wellesley College

#5 ALLOCATED MAINTENANCE COSTS TO GIFT TYPE

(A) Year	(B) Maintenance Dollars W/S #2 Col F	(C) Gift Annuities Estimate %	(D) $ (BxC)	(E) Pooled Income Estimate %	(F) $ (BxE)	(G) Annuity Trusts Estimate %	(H) $ (BxG)	(I) Unitrusts Estimate %	(J) $ (BxI)
(Example Years)									
~~1979~~									
1978	$46,100	26%	$11,986	37%	$17,057			37%	$17,057
1977	$35,200	26%	$9,152	37%	$13,024			37%	$13,024
1976	$35,500	26%	$9,230	37%	$13,135			37%	$13,135
~~1975~~									

NOTE: Amount in Column B must equal sum of amounts in Columns D, F, H, and J.

188

Wellesley College

#6 PROJECTED MAINTENANCE COSTS

(A) Year	(B) Total Dollars Under Management — Historical records	(C) Total Costs — W/S #5 Col D, F, H or J	(D) Cost Per Dollar Under Management — Col C ÷ Col B
(Example Years) ~~1979~~			
1978	$837,000	$11,986	$.01
1977	$613,000	$9,152	$.01
1976	$218,000	$9,230	$.04
~~1975~~			

(E) Future Years	(F) Projected Cost Per Dollar Under Management — Best estimate which corresponds to values in Col D. Adjust for projected inflation rate (Reference Table 6.2.1)	(G) Projected Dollars Under Management — Use Beginning of Year Balance from worksheet #10 or #11 as appropriate	(H) Projected Annual Maintenance Costs (FxG)
1978-1	$.01	$837,000	$8,370
1979-2	.01	803,426	8,034
1980-3	.01	764,930	7,649
1981-4	.01	735,180	7,352
1982-5	.01	710,767	7,108
1983-6	.02	689,990	13,780
1984-7	.02	669,089	13,382
1985-8	.02	646,633	12,933
1986-9	.02	620,148	12,403
1987-10	.02	597,608	11,752
1988-11	.02	547,736	10,955
1989-12	.02	507,534	10,151
1990-13	.02	467,452	9,349
1991-14	.02	427,355	8,547
1992-15	.03	388,026	11,641
1993-16	.03	349,521	10,486
1994-17	.03	311,877	9,356
1995-18	.03	275,624	8,269
1996-19	.03	241,461	7,244
1997-20	.03	209,565	6,287

(Check one)

✓ Gift Annuities
___ Pooled Income
___ Annuity Trusts
___ Unitrusts

ERNST & WHINNEY
COST/BENEFIT ANALYSIS WORKSHEETS
ANNUITY, CHARITABLE TRUST AND BEQUEST PROGRAM
AS OF JUNE 30, 19____

Wellesley College

DONOR DATA

(A) Unique Number	(B) Date	(C) Amount (Dollars)	(D) %	(E) Dollars	(F) Date of Birth	(G) Attained Age	(H) Gift Dollars Weighted by Age
		Agreement Information		Payout	Donor and Beneficiary Information		
Assign a unique number, preferably sequential, to each agreement	Record the date agreement was signed	Note the original gift value	Agreed payout percentage (if available)	State every agreed payout in dollars	For each payee	Age (to the nearest birthday) on date this calculation is made	(CxG)

(Check one)

✓ Gift Annuities
___ Annuity Trusts
___ Unitrusts

82. *Last Agreement #*

86. *Last Payee D.O.B.*

| Totals | | $937,000 | | $60,697 | | | $63,289,000 |

Computation of Factors: Number of Lives per Agreement = Total Number of Payees (Column F) ÷ Total Number of Agreements (Column A) = $86 \div 82 = 1.04$

Weighted Average Payout Rate = (Total Amount in Column E ÷ Total Amount in Column C) X 100 = 7.25 %.

Weighted Average Age = Total in Column H ÷ Total in Column C = 75.6 years.

Note: In Column A, several agreements may be lumped together as one agreement if they became effective in the same tax year and included identical terms and payees – or if the new agreements were simply additions to trusts already in existence from prior tax years.

ERNST & WHINNEY
COST/BENEFIT ANALYSIS WORKSHEETS
ANNUITY, CHARITABLE TRUST AND BEQUEST PROGRAM
AS OF JUNE 30, 19____

Wellesley College

#9 BOOK VALUE (The market value of each asset in an agreement at the time the asset was acquired by purchase or as a gift)

(Check one):
- ✓ Gift Annuities
- ___ Annuity Trusts
- ___ Unitrusts (including pre-1969 trusts, tax-exempt income trusts, basic-fixed %, and net income or income-only unitrusts)

(A) Year	(B) Beginning of Year Balance	(C) Rate	(D) Payout (Dollars)	(E) Mortality Release Factor	(F) Value Released Dollars	(G) Investment Income Rate (%)	(H) Investment Income (Dollars)	(I) End of Year Balance
Year 1: fiscal year in which this calculation is being made	Year 1: obtain from records Years 2-20: Carry forward from Col I	Weighted Average Payout Rate W/S #7	(BxC)	Select factors from Reference Table 6.2.2 most closely associated with the Number of Lives per Agreement on W/S #7 and Weighted Average Age on W/S #7	(BxE)	See Table 6.2.3	(BxG)	(B-D-F+H)
1	$837,000	7 1/4 %	$60,683	* 3.735	$31,242	6.30 %	$52,731	$797,786
2	797,786		57,839	4.517	36,036	6.30	50,261	754,172
3	754,172		54,677	5.043	38,033	6.30	47,513	708,975
4	708,975		51,401	5.522	39,150	6.30	44,665	663,089
5	663,089		48,074	5.985	39,686	6.30	41,775	617,104
6	617,104		44,740	6.446	39,779	6.57	40,544	573,129
7	573,129		41,552	6.909	39,557	6.83	39,145	531,125
8	531,125		38,507	7.381	39,202	7.07	37,551	490,967
9	490,967		35,595	7.844	38,610	7.30	35,841	452,603
10	452,603		32,814	8.362	37,847	7.51	33,990	415,932
11	415,932		30,155	8.877	36,922	7.72	32,110	380,965
12	380,965		27,620	9.410	35,849	7.93	30,211	347,707
13	347,707		25,209	9.963	34,642	8.14	28,303	316,159
14	316,159		22,922	10.536	33,311	8.33	26,336	286,262
15	286,262		20,754	11.131	31,864	8.52	24,390	258,034
16	258,034		18,707	11.748	30,314	8.46	21,830	230,843
17	230,843		16,736	12.388	28,597	8.40	19,391	204,901
18	204,901		14,855	13.051	26,742	8.35	17,109	180,413
19	180,413		13,080	13.739	24,787	8.30	14,974	157,520
20	157,520		11,420	14.454	22,728	8.25	13,995	136,327

* Used 1.1 Lives per Agreement and 77 as weighted average age.

ERNST & WHINNEY
COST/BENEFIT ANALYSIS WORKSHEETS
ANNUITY, CHARITABLE TRUST AND BEQUEST PROGRAM
AS OF JUNE 30, 19___

Wellesley College

#10 FAIR MARKET VALUE (Market value of each asset in an agreement as of the date six months after the beginning of the current fiscal year)

(Check one)
✓ Gift Annuities
___ Annuity Trusts

(A) Year	(B) Beginning of Year Balance	(C) Book Value Released	(D) Book Value To Fair Market Value Ratio	(E) Fair Market Value Factor	(F) Releases at Fair Market Value	(G) End of Year Balance
Year 1: fiscal year 1980 (Example Years)	Year 1: obtain from records Years 2-20: Carry forward from Col G	Use values in W/S #9 Col F	Divide value in Col B by value in W/S #9 Col B for the same year	Reference Table 6.2.4 adjusted to end of the fiscal year	(CxDxE)	(BxE) - (F) - W/S #9 Col D + W/S #9 Col H
1	$ 837,000	$ 31,262	1.0	1.007	$ 31,481	$ 803,426
2	803,426	36,036	1.007	1.007	36,542	764,930
3	764,930	38,033	1.014	1.022	39,414	735,180
4	735,180	39,150	1.037	1.033	41,938	710,767
5	710,767	39,496	1.072	1.042	44,330	689,990
6	689,990	39,779	1.118	1.043	46,385	669,089
7	669,089	39,597	1.167	1.042	48,151	646,633
8	646,633	39,202	1.217	1.037	49,474	620,128
9	620,128	38,610	1.263	1.028	50,130	587,608
10	587,608	37,847	1.299	1.015	49,842	547,736
11	547,736	36,922	1.317	1.013	49,258	507,554
12	507,554	35,849	1.332	1.011	48,272	467,452
13	467,452	34,642	1.344	1.008	46,931	427,355
14	427,355	33,311	1.352	1.006	45,307	389,026
15	388,026	31,864	1.355	1.003	43,305	349,521
16	349,521	30,314	1.355	1.001	41,117	311,877
17	311,877	28,597	1.351	.999	39,596	275,624
18	275,624	26,742	1.345	.998	35,866	241,461
19	241,461	24,787	1.338	.997	33,066	209,565
20	209,565	22,768	1.330	.997	30,191	180,320

ERNST & WHINNEY
COST/BENEFIT ANALYSIS WORKSHEETS
ANNUITY, CHARITABLE TRUST AND BEQUEST PROGRAM
AS OF JUNE 30, 19___

Wellesley College

#12 TOTAL PROJECTED BENEFITS

(A)	(B)	(C) GIFT ANNUITIES	(D)	(E)	(F) TRUSTS AND POOLED INCOME FUNDS	(G)	(H)
			RELEASES AT FAIR MARKET VALUE				
Year	Payout	Investment Income	Releases At Fair Market Value	TOTAL	Pooled Income	Annuity Trusts	Unitrusts
	W/S #9 Col D	W/S #9 Col H	W/S #10 Col F	(C+D-B)	W/S #11 Col E	W/S #10 Col F	W/S #11 Col E
1	($ 60,683)	$ 52,731	$ 31,481	$ 23,529	$	$	$
2	(57,839)	50,261	36,542	28,964			
3	(54,677)	47,513	39,414	32,250			
4	(51,401)	44,665	41,938	35,202			
5	(48,074)	41,775	44,330	38,031			
6	(44,740)	40,544	46,385	42,189			
7	(41,552)	39,145	48,151	45,744			
8	(38,507)	37,551	48,474	48,518			
9	(35,595)	35,841	50,130	50,376			
10	(32,814)	33,990	49,862	51,038			
11	(30,155)	32,110	49,258	51,213			
12	(27,620)	30,211	48,276	50,867			
13	(25,209)	28,303	46,931	50,025			
14	(22,922)	26,336	45,307	48,721			
15	(20,754)	24,390	43,805	46,941			
16	(18,707)	21,830	41,117	44,240			
17	(16,736)	18,291	38,596	41,251			
18	(14,855)	17,109	35,866	38,140			
19	(13,080)	14,974	33,066	34,960			
20	(11,420)	12,995	30,191	31,766			

193

ERNST & WHINNEY
COST/BENEFIT ANALYSIS WORKSHEETS
ANNUITY, CHARITABLE TRUST AND BEQUEST PROGRAM
AS OF JUNE 30, 19____

Wellesley College

#13   CALCULATION OF INTERNAL RATE OF RETURN

Internal rate of return (IRR) is an interest rate that equates the present value of a set of cash flows with an initial investment. It is the interest rate that is obtained when the calculated net present value of a series of cash flows is zero. IRR is also called the yield or discounted rate of return. IRR has been programmed into many hand-held calculators. The method for computing IRR and the accompanying Present Value Tables are found in standard financial management texts such as <u>Managerial Finance</u>, Weston & Brigham, Holt, Rinehart and Winston, 1981.

(Check one)

✓   Gift Annuities
___ Pooled Income
___ Annuity Trusts
___ Unitrusts

(A) Year	(B) Historical Cultivation and Solicitation Costs W/S #4	(C) Projected Annual Agreement Maintenance Costs W/S #6 Col H	(D) Projected Benefits W/S #12 Col E, F, G or H	(E) Annual Cash Flow Stream Year 0 = all C&S costs Years 1-20 = (D-C)
0	($78,687)			($78,687)
1		$8,370	$23,549	$15,159
2		$8,034	$28,964	$20,930
3		7,649	32,250	24,601
4		7,352	35,202	27,850
5		7,108	38,031	30,923
6		13,780	42,189	28,409
7		13,382	45,744	32,362
8		12,933	48,518	35,575
9		12,403	50,376	37,973
10		11,752	51,039	39,286
11		10,955	51,213	40,258
12		10,151	50,867	40,716
13		9,349	50,025	40,676
14		8,547	48,721	40,174
15		11,641	46,941	35,300
16		10,486	44,240	33,754
17		9,356	41,251	31,895
18		8,269	38,120	29,851
19		7,244	34,960	27,716
20		6,287	31,766	25,479

To perform IRR: Utilize (E) and assume remaining balance will be received evenly over years 21-30.

IRR. Stream of benefits in (Column E) represent an internal rate of return of 3.9% and 3.2%.

Remaining Balance

ERNST & WHINNEY
COST/BENEFIT ANALYSIS WORKSHEETS
ANNUITY, CHARITABLE TRUST AND BEQUEST PROGRAM
AS OF JUNE 30, 19___

Wellesley College

#15   CALCULATION OF OVERALL IRR

(A)	(B)	(C)	(D)	(E)	(F)	(G)
	Gift Annuities	Pooled Income*	Annuity Trusts	Unitrusts*	Outright Bequests	Total Annual Cash Flow Stream
			ANNUAL CASH FLOW STREAMS			
Year	W/S #13 Col E	W/S #13 Col E	W/S #13 Col E	W/S #13 Col E	W/S #14 Col D	
0	($ 78,687)	($ 80,019)	($)	($ 4,250)	$	($ 163,356)
1	$ 15,139	$ 27,533	$	$ 17,954	$	$ 60,646
2	20,930	35,052		34,268		90,254
3	24,601	39,173		44,144		107,918
4	27,850	42,973		52,128		122,851
5	30,923	46,346		59,205		136,474
6	28,409	38,988		52,035		119,432
7	32,362	42,278		57,534		132,197
8	35,595	45,204		61,931		142,720
9	37,973	47,536		64,715		150,234
10	39,281	48,863		66,186		154,335
11	40,258	49,387		67,084		156,729
12	40,716	49,736		67,147		157,589
13	40,676	49,704		66,460		156,840
14	40,199	49,324		65,048		154,546
15	35,300	43,330		55,892		133,522
16	33,754	41,769		54,132		129,655
17	31,895	40,749		51,598		124,242
18	29,851	39,307		48,677		117,835
19	27,716	37,375		45,404		110,495
20	25,479	35,140		41,931		102,550

Remaining Balance $ _____

To Perform IRR: Utilize (G) and assume
remaining balance will be received evenly
over years 21-30.

* Existing calculation for Pooled Fund and Unitrust generate flow not Trust included.

IRR: stream of benefit in (Col E) repres. its annual rate of return of 55% - 57%/yr.

INTERNAL RATE OF RETURN CALCULATIONS

GRINNELL COLLEGE

WORKSHEETS

# 1	Omitted.
# 2	Five-year history of costs was submitted.
# 3	Omitted.
# 4	Omitted.
Unnumbered	Summary of New Agreements and Adjusted Costs
#5 - #14	Omitted.
#15	Supporting calculations have not been included.

Original worksheet formats were used and do not include modifications shown in Section 6.1.5.

196

ERNST & WHINNEY
COST/BENEFIT ANALYSIS WORKSHEETS
ANNUITY, CHARITABLE TRUST AND BEQUEST PROGRAM
AS OF JUNE 30, 19___

Grinnell College

#2   ALLOCATED COSTS
CULTIVATION AND SOLICITATION/MAINTENANCE

(A) Year	(B) Total A&T Dollars W/S #1	(C) Cultivation & % Estimate	(D) Solicitation $ (BxC)	(E) Maintenance % Estimate	(F) $ (BxE)	Total %
(Example Years)						100%
1980	$ 117,695	65%	$ 76,502	35%	$ 41,193	
1979	$ 94,711	65%	$ 61,562	35%	$ 33,149	
1978	$ 84,029	65%	$ 54,619	35%	$ 29,410	
1977	$ 41,348	65%	$ 26,876	35%	$ 14,472	
1976	$ 40,624	65%	$ 26,406	35%	$ 14,218	
~~1975~~						

197

SUMMARY OF GRINNELL COLLEGE AGREEMENTS

HISTORICAL C&S COSTS
ALL AGREEMENT TYPES

NUMBER OF NEW AGREEMENTS

Year	Gift Annuity	Pooled Fund	Annuity Trust	Unitrust
1980	1	6	—	4
1979	6	1	3	3
1978	—	3	1	4
1977	2	5	4	2
1976	1	2	2	1
Agreements in Force	10	17	10	14
Total C&S Costs Adjusted for Inflation to 1980 Dollars	$18,305	$33,095	$18,208	$31,160

ERNST & WHINNEY
COST/BENEFIT ANALYSIS WORKSHEETS
ANNUITY, CHARITABLE TRUST AND BEQUEST PROGRAM
AS OF JUNE 30, 19___

Grinnell College

#15   CALCULATION OF OVERALL IRR

(A)	(B)	(C)	(D) ANNUAL CASH FLOW STREAMS	(E)	(F)	(G)	*Without Bequests*
Year	Gift Annuities	Pooled Income	Annuity Trusts	Unitrusts	Outright Bequests	Total Annual Cash Flow Stream	
	W/S #13 Col E	W/S #13 Col E	W/S #13 Col E	W/S #13 Col E	W/S #14 Col D		
0	($ 8,305)	($ 33,095)	($ 18,208)	($ 31,160)		($ 100,768)	
1	($ 3,658)	($ 3,016)	$ 31,973	$ 54,980	$ 217,662	$ 297,941	$ 80,279
2	(1,479)	2,015	78,442	98,959	217,662	381,269	163,607
3	(1,845)	2,331	113,736	111,424	217,662	438,646	220,984
4	(210)	1,688	144,258	129,562	217,662	489,584	271,922
5	1,202	1,117	167,762	142,502	217,662	528,211	310,549
6	2,627	1,548	192,861	156,381	217,662	507,983	350,321
7	2,677	1,055	211,248	165,114	217,662	576,766	359,104
8	3,447	576	226,199	171,221	217,662	617,923	400,261
9	4,141	1,055	240,073	176,398	217,662	637,219	418,357
10	4,326	647	245,550	175,551	217,662	642,442	424,780
11	3,721	1,077	253,776	175,925	217,662	649,007	431,345
12	3,943	600	253,316	172,174	217,662	646,495	428,823
13	3,940	161	252,542	167,073	217,662	641,056	423,394
14	3,301	430	251,904	162,527	217,662	635,024	417,362
15	3,233	18	246,173	155,050	217,662	622,100	404,438
16	3,057	219	238,925	146,750	217,662	606,175	388,513
17	2,469	143	228,453	137,139	217,662	605,587	387,925
18	2,241	7	218,467	128,182	217,662	566,545	348,883
19	1,753	109	204,781	117,559	217,662	541,645	323,983
20	1,537	179	190,194	106,911	217,662	516,423	298,821

Remaining Balance $ _____ $ _____

To Perform IRR: Utilize (G) and assume
remaining balance will be received evenly
over years 21-30.

Note: IRR over 100%
Probable range 100%-150%
Details supporting calculation
for each form of payment are
not included.

APPENDIX C

Procedures for Life Income Trust Program at the University of Pennsylvania

University of Pennsylvania Procedures

I. *Prior to Settlement:*
A. Planned Giving Office will:
  1. Determine and negotiate terms of Agreement within guidelines of Ad Hoc Trustee Committee on Planned Gifts.
     (e.g., minimum gift, minimum age of beneficiary, and percentage payout required, minimum 5%).
  2. Where necessary, exceptions to guidelines will be made with consent of Ad Hoc Committee on Planned Gifts and Investment Board.
  3. Determine nature of appropriate form of Agreement:
     a. Unitrust
     b. Annuity trust
     c. Pooled life income fund
     d. Gift annuity
     e. Deferred gift annuity
     f. Charitable lead trust
  4. Determine source of funds for:
     a. Agent and custodian fees
     b. Investment adviser fees
     c. Appraisal fees, if applicable
  5. Determine nature of gift property to be conveyed by Settlor, e.g.:
     a. Description
     b. Market value
     c. Method of acquisition
     d. Date of acquisition
     e. Date of gift
     f. Payment schedule

6. Determine Settlor's tax basis of gift property to be conveyed.
7. Obtain *pro forma* portfolio of trust from Investment Board.*
8. Calculate and report to Settlor:
   a. Approximate remainder interest factor or charitable deduction.
   b. Approximate gift tax requirement.
   c. *Pro forma* portfolio, when applicable.
9. Determine, where appropriate, Settlor's (and Beneficiary's, if other than Settlor):
   a. Legal Counsel
   b. Trust Adviser
   c. Investment Counsel or Broker
   d. Tax Adviser
10. Prepare, with advice of Counsel, Development Program, Agreement in seven or more copies as required:
    a. Original for Treasurer's Office
    b. 2d counterpart for Settlor
    c. 3d counterpart for Counsel, Development Program
    d. 4th counterpart for Agent and Custodian
    e. 5th counterpart for Life Income Trust Officer of Planned Giving Program
    f. 6th counterpart for Investment Adviser
    g. 7th (etc.) counterpart for Beneficiary (if other than Settlor); for Settlor's and/or Beneficiary's Legal Counsel, if appropriate
11. Determine:
    a. *Settlor's*
       1a. Name
       2a. Date of birth
       3a. Sex
       4a. Social Security number

---

* Using such agents as the Investment Board might choose.

   5a. Address
   6a. Telephone number
  b. *Beneficiary's* (if other than settlor)
   1b. Name
   2b. Date of birth
   3b. Sex
   4b. Social Security number
   5b. Address
   6b. Telephone number
   7b. Relationship to donor
  12. Determine valuation date
  13. Coordinate with Treasurer's Office

II. *At Settlement*:
 A. Planned Giving Office will:
  1. Present required number of copies of Agreement for execution by Settlor.
  2. Secure delivery of assets given or appropriate evidence of same.
  3. List property in detail.
  4. Xerox certificates, powers, deeds, policies, and checks conveyed.
  5. Have "Schedule A" typed, initialed by Treasurer and Settlor, and appended to Agreement.
  6. Take custody of Agreement.
  7. Have the attest and seal affixed by the Secretary.

III. *After Settlement*:
 A. Planned Giving Office will:
  1. Deliver original to Treasurer's Office and one or more executed counterparts to relevant parties and their advisers, Agent and Custodian, Investment Board.
  2. Write Agent and Custodian—with copies to appropriate parties:
   a. Enclosing copy of Agreement.
   b. Supplying Settlor's basis of each item.
   c. Advising with respect to short and full fiscal year.
   d. Advising with respect to:

1d. Settlor's .... Date of birth
                                  Sex
                                  Social Security
                                    number
                                  Address

2d. Beneficiary's .... Date of birth
    (if other than Settlor)   Sex
                                  Social Security
                                    number
                                  Address

  3. Deliver property to Treasurer.

B. Treasurer will:

  1. Ascertain market value or appraise property conveyed, including accrued interest if any.

  2. Confer with Investment Board with respect to sale or retention of securities in consultation with Life Income Trust Officer.

  3. Record gift and open trust fund account in university's system.

  4. Prepare and deliver to Life Income Trust Officer university's formal gift receipt.

  5. Deliver university's formal gift receipt and copy of "Schedule A" to Life Income Trust Officer for transmission to Settlor.

C. Agent and Custodian will:

  1. Provide Treasurer with safekeeping receipt for property delivered thereto.

  2. Transfer into name of university nominee registered items to be retained.

3. *Trusts*	3. *Pooled Life Income Fund*
a. Assign account number to new Trust.	a. Compute number of units assigned.

b. Apply to IRS for tax exempt identification number for new Trust.

c. Calculate distribution payable for short fiscal year.

d. Advise Treasurer and Life Income Trust Officer concerning the above.

b. Advise Treasurer and Life Income Trust Officer.

D. Investment Board will:
   1. Determine an appropriate investment program being mindful of:
      a. The nature of the Agreement;
      b. The Settlor's objectives in creating the trust;
      c. Potential future gifts to the university by the Settlor;
      d. Personal property and other nuisance taxes;
      e. Market conditions, etc.
   2. Issue buy and sell instructions to Custodian.

E. Agent and Custodian in due course will:
   1. Place orders for securities; transactions.
   2. Send Life Income Trust Officer and Treasurer financial statements of account, monthly or quarterly, as requested.
   3. Calculate and make payments of Pennsylvania Personal Property Tax and Pennsylvania Corporate Loan Tax, when applicable.
   4. Prepare and file annual tax returns: IRS Form 1041 and, if applicable, Pennsylvania Form 40.
   5. Send Life Income Trust Officer two copies of IRS Form 1041 and, if applicable, Pennsylvania Form 40 for each requisite period.

6. *Trusts*

    a. Send required beneficiary distributions to Life Income Trust Officer by check to be signed by Treasurer and forwarded to Beneficiaries.

    b. For Unitrusts, calculate annual distributions payable as of each valuation date and advise Investment Board and Life Income Trust Officer.

6. *Pooled Life Income Fund*

    a. Calculate income allocable to each Beneficiary and send distribution to Life Income Trust Officer by check to be signed by Treasurer and forwarded to Beneficiary.

    b. Calculate Fund's annual rate of return at close of fiscal year and advise Investment Board, Treasurer and Life Income Trust Officer.

    c. Send Life Income Trust Officer data needed for annual report to be compiled by university's auditors.

F. Life Income Trust Officer will:
    1. Attend to mailing and delivery of:
       a. Income payments
       b. Financial statements, as appropriate.
       c. IRS Form 1041 and, if applicable, Pennsylvania Form 40.
       d. Annual Reports.

2. Prepare and deliver to Investment Board and Treasurer an annual statement of assets and liabilities, income and expense of each Trust on its valuation day, or as soon thereafter as possible.
3. Continue liaison with the Settlor and Beneficiaries.
4. Alert Director of Life Income Trusts to additional gift potential of program participants.

NOTES: A special manual will be developed by the Planned Giving Office outlining procedures to be followed when admitting new funds to the Pooled Life Income Fund, and of withdrawing such upon the death of the Settlor or the surviving Life Interest therein. A special manual will be developed by the Planned Giving Office outlining procedures to be followed for trusts funded with special gifts which include life insurance, real estate, art, and other personal property.

Agreement Forms for the Pomona Plan

Typical Forms Between Donors and Pomona College

This appendix includes typical forms for agreements between donors and Pomona College. These forms were prepared by the college's attorneys and were in use at the time the Ernst & Whinney portion of the study was initiated. This sampling of Pomona College forms is provided for illustrative purposes only and not as a guide to the preparation of such documents.

These are important legal documents that should be prepared by attorneys who represent the institution and who are conversant with the applicable state laws. Pomona College has encouraged its donors to have their attorneys review the agreement forms and to seek a private letter ruling in instances in which the donor's attorney proposes substantive changes to the language proposed by the college.

Annuity Trust Agreement

_____, hereinafter referred to as "the Donor," does hereby transfer, deliver, and give in trust to POMONA COLLEGE, a California nonprofit corporation, hereinafter referred to as "the Trustee," the property described on the separate schedule attached hereto and marked "Exhibit A." The Trustee accepts said property at the net fair market value of $_____. Such property, together with any other property that may later become subject to this trust, shall constitute the trust estate, and shall be held, managed, and distributed as hereinafter provided.

A. *Distribution of Income and Principal*
1. The Trustee shall distribute in each taxable year of the trust to the Donor during his lifetime, and thereafter to his wife, _____, hereinafter sometimes called "the Beneficiary," during her lifetime if she survives him, an annuity amount equal to _____ percent (_____%) of the initial net fair market value of the trust assets as finally determined for federal tax purposes. The annuity amount shall be reduced for a short taxable year, as hereinafter provided. The annuity amount shall be paid in equal quarterly installments at the end of each calendar quarter from income and, to the extent that income is not sufficient, from principal. Any income of the trust for a taxable year in excess of the annuity amount shall be added to principal. The annuity amount may be distributed in cash or in other property.
2. The obligation of the Trustee to pay the annuity amount to the Donor or the beneficiary shall terminate with the regular payment next preceding the death of such person, and the annuity amount accrued from the date of such payment shall be distributed to the owner of the next successive beneficial interest hereunder.
3. If the initial net fair market value of the trust assets is incorrectly determined by the Trustee, then within a reasonable period after the final determination of the correct value, the Trustee shall pay to the proper recipient in the case of an

undervaluation or shall receive from the proper recipient in the case of an overvaluation an amount equal to the difference between the annuity amount properly payable and the annuity amount actually paid.

4. The first taxable year of this trust shall commence with the date of the execution of this agreement and subsequent taxable years shall commence on the first day of January each year.

5. In determining the annuity amount for a short taxable year and for the taxable year in which the trust terminates pursuant to the provisions of subparagraph 6 or subparagraph 7 below of this paragraph A, the Trustee shall prorate the same on a daily basis.

6. The Donor hereby expressly reserves the power, exercisable only by last Will, to revoke and terminate all, but not less than all, of the rights of the beneficiary under this trust, and in the event that all of such rights of the beneficiary are so terminated, then upon the death of the Donor this trust shall terminate.

7. Unless terminated at an earlier date under the foregoing provisions, this trust shall terminate upon the death of the survivor of the Donor and the beneficiary, and within a reasonable time after the termination of this trust, the Trustee shall distribute all of the remaining principal and income of this trust to Pomona College to be used in accordance with the wishes of the Donor as set forth in the separate schedule attached hereto and marked "Exhibit B."

8. If at the date of the termination of this trust, Pomona College is not an organization described in Sections 170(c), 2055(a), and 2522(a) of the Internal Revenue Code of 1954 (or any substitute provisions), the property no longer subject to this trust shall instead be distributed upon similar terms and conditions to one or more similar organizations then so described as the Trustee shall select in its sole discretion and in such shares as it shall determine.

B. *Powers of the Trustee*

To carry out the purposes of this trust and subject to any limitations stated elsewhere in this agreement, the Trustee is vested with the following powers, in addition to any now or hereafter conferred by law, affecting the trust or the trust estate:

1. To continue to hold any property received by the trust, and to operate at the risk of the trust estate any business received or acquired by it, as long as the Trustee shall deem it advisable.

2. To manage, control, sell, convey, exchange, partition, divide, subdivide, develop, improve, repair, or abandon a trust asset or any interest therein; to grant options and to sell upon deferred payments; to lease for terms within or extending beyond the duration of this trust for any purpose, including exploration for and removal of gas, oil, and other minerals; to enter into community oil leases, pooling and unitization agreements; to amend or extend existing leases; to create restrictions, easements, and other servitudes; to compromise, arbitrate, or otherwise adjust claims in favor of or against the trust; to institute, compromise, and defend actions and proceedings; to carry such insurance as the Trustee may deem advisable.

3. To invest and reinvest the principal, and the income if accumulated, in such property as the Trustee may deem advisable, whether or not of the character permitted by law for the investment of trust funds, including property in which the Trustee owns an undivided interest in any other trust capacity.

4. To loan or advance its own funds to this trust for any trust purpose, and any such loan or advance shall be a first lien against the trust assets and shall be repaid therefrom without interest; to set up reserves out of income for the payment of taxes, assessments, insurance, repairs, fees, and other expenses of the trust.

5. To borrow money for any trust purpose upon such terms and conditions as the Trustee may deem proper, and to obligate the trust estate for repayment; to encumber the trust estate or any of its property by mortgage, deed of trust, pledge or otherwise, using such procedure to consummate the transaction as the Trustee may deem advisable; and to replace, renew, or extend any encumbrance upon any trust property.

6. To have respecting securities all the rights, powers and privileges of an owner, including the power to vote, give general or limited proxies, and pay assessments and other sums deemed by the Trustee necessary for the protection of the trust estate; to participate in voting trusts, pooling agreements, foreclosures, reorganizations, consolidations, mergers, and liquidations, and in connection therewith to deposit securities with and transfer title to any protective or other committee under such terms as the Trustee may deem advisable; to exercise or sell stock subscription or conversion rights; to accept and retain as an investment any securities or other property

received through the exercise of any of the foregoing powers; and to hold securities or other property in the name of the Trustee, in the name of a nominee of the Trustee, or in the name of a custodian (or its nominee) selected by the Trustee, with or without disclosure of this trust, the Trustee being responsible for the acts of such custodian or nominee affecting such property.

7. In determining what is income or principal and the expenses that shall be charged to either account, the Trustee shall be governed by the provisions of the California Principal and Income Law as its exists from time to time, but if any matter related to such determination is not provided for in this agreement or in said law, the Trustee shall have full power and authority to determine such matter. Notwithstanding any other provision herein, if any pronouncements of the United States Treasury Department or the Internal Revenue Service shall require allocations between principal and income different from those provided by the California Principal and Income Law, the Trustee may allocate between principal and income in accordance with said pronouncements.

8. A material purpose in establishing this trust is to obtain the charitable deduction allowable pursuant to the provisions of the Internal Revenue Code or other similar statute in force from time to time. The Trustee is, therefore, expressly authorized to enter into any and all agreements with the Internal Revenue Service or any other governmental body or official or to execute, from time to time, any declarations of policy or disclaimers restricting the discretion given it in order to preserve the charitable deduction provided for herein. Moreover, the Trustee shall exercise all powers and discretions only in a manner consistent with the allowance of all federal charitable tax deductions to which the Donor, or the estate of the Donor, may otherwise be entitled under the provisions of the Internal Revenue Code.

9. Nothing in this trust shall be construed to restrict the Trustee from investing the trust assets in a manner which could result in the annual realization of a reasonable amount of income or gain from the sale or disposition of trust assets.

10. Except for the payments expressly required under paragraph A above, the Trustee is prohibited from engaging in any act of self-dealing as defined in Section 4941(d) of the Internal Revenue Code of 1954 and from making any taxable ex-

penditure as defined in Section 4945(d) of said Code, not-withstanding any other provision in this instrument to the contrary.

C. *No Additions to Trust Estate*
No future contributions may be made to this trust after the initial contribution.

D. *Revocation and Amendment*
This trust is irrevocable and shall not be subject to amendment or modification. Provided, however, that the Trustee shall have the power to amend this trust to the extent permitted by the regulations promulgated by the Department of the Treasury pursuant to Section 664 of the Internal Revenue Code of 1954 for the sole purpose of qualifying this trust as a charitable remainder trust as defined by Section 664 of the Code (or any substitute provision).

E. *General Provisions*
   1. In the event of the incompetence of the Donor or the beneficiary, each distribution required hereunder may, at the sole discretion of the Trustee, be made without the intervention of a guardian or a conservator; or the Trustee may make such distribution for the benefit of the recipient, or the Trustee may distribute to a guardian or a conservator. The Trustee shall not be required to see to the application of any such payments so made to any of said persons, but such payees' receipts therefor shall be a full discharge to the Trustee.
   2. The Trustee shall have the right to resign at any time, and upon such resignation the Trustee or any beneficiary of the trust may secure the appointment of a successor Trustee by a court of competent jurisdiction, at the expense of the trust. Each successor Trustee must be a corporation or national banking association authorized to conduct the business of a trust company in California. Each Trustee shall be responsible only for its own actions or omissions as Trustee. No successor Trustee shall be required to audit or investigate the acts or administration of any prior Trustee and shall be relieved of all liability therefor. Each successor Trustee shall be vested with all the title, rights, powers, discretions, privileges, duties, and obligations of the original Trustee.
   3. Pomona College shall receive no compensation for its ordinary services as Trustee but shall be entitled to receive reimbursement of reasonable expenses incurred in discharging the duties of Trustee. Any successor Trustee shall be entitled to reason-

able compensation for its services not in excess of the compensation normally charged by it to administer similar accounts.

4. The Donor hereby agrees to provide, by Will or otherwise, that any death tax attributable to assets held in the trust at the Donor's death shall be paid from sources other than the trust.

5. This trust has been accepted by the Trustee and will be administered in the State of California, and its validity, construction and all rights thereunder shall be governed by the laws of that State.

IN WITNESS WHEREOF, the parties hereto have executed this Annuity Trust Agreement this _____ day of _____, 19____.

_____

(Donor)

POMONA COLLEGE, Trustee

By _____
                Treasurer

By _____
              Assistant Treasurer

Exhibit A

The property given and transferred to Pomona College under the attached Annuity Trust Agreement with _____ consists of the following:

_____
(Name of Donor)

Exhibit B

The property released to Pomona College under the provisions of the attached Annuity Trust Agreement with _____ shall be applied to the following uses and purposes:

_____
(Name of Donor)

Unitrust Agreement

_____, hereinafter referred to as "the Donor," does hereby transfer, deliver and give in trust to POMONA COLLEGE, a California nonprofit corporation, hereinafter referred to as "the Trustee," the property described on the separate schedule attached hereto and marked "Exhibit A." The Trustee accepts said property, which, together with any other property that may later become subject to this trust, is hereinafter referred to as "the trust estate," and the Trustee agrees to hold, manage, and distribute the trust estate as hereinafter provided.

A. *Distribution of Income and Principal*
　1. The Trustee shall distribute in each taxable year of the trust to the Donor during his lifetime, a unitrust amount equal to (a) the trust income for such taxable year (as defined in Section 643(b) of the Internal Revenue Code of 1954 and the Regulations thereunder) or (b) _____ percent (_____%) of the net fair market value of the trust assets valued as of the first day of such taxable year, whichever is less. The unitrust amount shall be reduced for a short taxable year, and shall be increased for any taxable year in which there are additional contributions, as hereinafter provided. For any taxable year in which the trust income exceeds the amount determined above, the payments to be made under the above provisions shall also include such excess income to the extent that the aggregate of the amounts paid in previous years was less than _____ percent (_____%) of the aggregate net fair market value of the trust assets for those years. The unitrust amount shall be paid in approximately equal quarterly payments at the end of each quarter, or within a reasonable period thereafter. Any income of the trust in excess of such payments shall be added to principal.
　2. The obligation of the Trustee to pay the unitrust amount

shall terminate with the regular payment date immediately preceding the date of the Donor's death.

3. If any additional contributions are made to the trust after the initial contribution, the unitrust amount for the taxable year in which the assets are added to the trust shall be _____percent (_____%) of the sum of (i) the net fair market value of trust assets (excluding the assets so added and any income from, or appreciation on, such assets) and (ii) that proportion of the value of the assets so added that was excluded under (i) which the number of days in the period which begins with the date of contribution and ends with the earlier of the last day of the taxable year or the termination of the trust pursuant to the provisions of subparagraph 7 below of this paragraph A bears to the number of days in the period which begins with the first day of such taxable year and ends with the earlier of the last day of such taxable year or the termination of the trust pursuant to the provisions of subparagraph 7 below of this paragraph A subject to the following provisions:

a. If the trust income (as defined in Section 643(b) of the Internal Revenue Code of 1954 and the Regulations thereunder) for the period which begins on the first day of such taxable year and ends with the earlier of the last day of such taxable year or the date on which the trust terminates pursuant to the provisions of subparagraph 7 below of this paragraph A is less than the unitrust amount as determined above in this subparagraph 3, then the unitrust amount to be distributed by the Trustee shall be limited to the amount of such income.

b. If the trust income as determined under (a) exceeds the unitrust amount as determined above in this subparagraph 3 the payments to be made in such taxable year shall also include such excess income to the extent that the aggregate of the amounts paid in previous years was less than _____percent (_____%) of the aggregate net fair market value of the trust assets for those years.

In the event there is no valuation date after the time of the additional contribution, the assets so added shall be valued at the time of contribution.

4. If the net fair market value of the trust assets is incorrectly determined by the Trustee for any taxable year, then within a reasonable period after the final determination of the correct value, the Trustee shall pay to the Donor in the case of an undervaluation or shall receive from the Donor in the case of an overvaluation an amount equal to the difference between the unitrust amount properly payable and the unitrust amount actually paid.

5. The first taxable year of this trust shall commence with the date of the execution of this agreement and subsequent taxable years shall commence on the first day of January each year.

6. In determining the unitrust amount for a short taxable year and for the taxable year in which the trust terminates pursuant to the provisions of subparagraph 7 below of this paragraph A, the Trustee shall prorate the same on a daily basis.

7. This trust shall terminate upon the death of the Donor, and within a reasonable time after the termination of this trust, the Trustee shall distribute all of the remaining principal and income of this trust to Pomona College to be used in accordance with the wishes of the Donor as set forth in the separate schedule attached hereto and marked "Exhibit B."

8. If at the date of the termination of this trust, Pomona College is not an organization described in Sections 170(c), 2055(a) and 2522(a) of the Internal Revenue Code of 1954 (or any substitute provisions), the property no longer subject to this trust shall instead be distributed upon similar terms and conditions to one or more similar organizations then so described as the Trustee shall select in its sole discretion and in such shares as it shall determine.

B. *Powers of the Trustee*

[This section contains exactly the same wording as Section

B Powers of the Trustee of the Annuity Trust Agreement included in this Appendix.]

C. *Additions to Trust Estate*

The Donor or any other person shall have the right at any time, either during lifetime or by Will, to add to this trust other property acceptable to the Trustee, which additional property, upon its receipt and acceptance by the Trustee, shall become a part of the trust estate.

D. *Revocation and Amendment*

This trust is irrevocable and shall not be subject to amendment or modification. Provided, however, that the Trustee shall have the power to amend this trust to the extent permitted by the regulations promulgated by the Department of the Treasury pursuant to Section 664 of the Internal Revenue Code of 1954 for the sole purpose of qualifying this trust as a charitable remainder trust as defined by Section 664 of the Code (or any substitute provision).

E. *General Provisions*

(This section contains exactly the same wording as Section E General Provisions of the Annuity Trust Agreement included in this Appendix.)

IN WITNESS WHEREOF, the parties hereto have executed this Unitrust Agreement this _____day of _____, 19__.

_____

(Donor)

POMONA COLLEGE, Trustee

By _____

Treasurer

By _____

Assistant Treasurer

Exhibit A

The property given and transferred to Pomona College under the attached Unitrust Agreement with _____ consists of the following:

_____

(Name of Donor)

Exhibit B

The property released to Pomona College under the provisions of the attached Unitrust Agreement with _____ shall be applied to the following uses and purposes:

_____

(Name of Donor)

Pooled Income Fund

This Pomona College Pooled Fund Life Income Agreement is entered into this _____ day of _____, 19_____, by _____ (hereinafter called "Donor") and POMONA COLLEGE, a California non-profit corporation (hereinafter called the "College.") The Donor hereby irrevocably gives, transfers and delivers to the College the following described property (hereinafter called the "Property") having a total net fair market value of $_____:

subject to the following terms and conditions:

1. The Property shall become part of the trust known as "Pomona College Pooled Income Fund" (hereinafter called "the Fund") and shall be invested and reinvested as part of the Fund under the terms and provisions of said Fund.

2. The College hereby allocates to the Property _____Units of the Fund.

3. The College shall pay income, as that term is defined in the Fund, to _____during her (his) lifetime, and upon the death of _____, then to _____ for her (his) lifetime, as provided by the terms and conditions of the Fund.

4. The above provisions notwithstanding, _____ may terminate only by last Will duly admitted to probate all but not less than all of the rights of _____ to receive the income from the Units in the Fund, and in the event that all of such rights of _____ are terminated in the manner provided above, then upon the death of _____, the Units in the Fund shall belong to Pomona College, and it shall be entitled to redeem such Units at that time.

5. Unless terminated at an earlier date under the foregoing provisions, then upon the death of the survivor of _____ and _____, all of the Units then held under this Agreement shall become the property of Pomona

College, as Remainderman, and shall be redeemed by the Fund, as set forth in the provisions of said Fund.

6. A copy of the provisions of the Fund is attached and marked "Exhibit A."

IN WITNESS WHEREOF, the undersigned have executed this Agreement as of the date first above written.

_____

(Donor)

POMONA COLLEGE, Trustee

By _____
Treasurer

By _____
Assistant Treasurer

Exhibit A

Pomona College as Trustee hereby creates a trust qualifying as a pooled income fund under the terms and conditions hereinafter set forth.

Article I
Description of Fund

Pomona College (referred to herein as "Trustee" or "Pomona") has established this trust, described as the Pomona College Pooled Income Fund (referred to herein as "the Fund" or "Trust") as a pooled income fund as defined in Section 642(c) (5) of the Internal Revenue Code of 1954 as it shall be amended from time to time (referred to herein as "the Code"). More specifically:

A. This fund is established exclusively for the management and investment of property transferred by donors who contribute an irrevocable remainder interest in such property to Pomona, an organization described in Section 170(b) (1) (A) (ii) of the Code, such donors retaining an income interest for the life of one or more beneficiaries living at the time such property is transferred to this trust.

B. Property transferred by each donor to the Fund shall be commingled with, and invested or reinvested with, property transferred by other donors who have made or make transfers described in paragraph A above.

C. This Fund shall not accept, as property transferred to it by any donor, and will not invest in, any security the income from which is exempt from federal income tax under subtitle A of the Code.

D. This Fund shall include only amounts received through transfers from donors described in this Article I.

E. This Fund shall continue to be maintained by Pomona as Trustee and Pomona shall be the sole remainderman with respect to property donated to the Fund: any person exercising general responsibilities with respect to this Fund which are ordinarily exercised by a trustee shall not be a donor or a beneficiary of any income interest in this Fund, provided, however, that Pomona may be a beneficiary of such an interest; and, each beneficiary of an income interest from this Fund shall receive, for each year in which the beneficiary is entitled to receive the income interest referred to in Article V hereinbelow, income determined by the rate of return earned by this Fund for such year.

ARTICLE II
Fiscal Year
The fiscal year of this Fund shall be the calendar year.

ARTICLE III
Value and Allocation of Units
A. ALLOCATION OF UNITS UPON INITIAL DONATIONS. For purposes of the initial donations to this Fund, one or more units of participation in the Fund (referred to herein as Units) shall be assigned to the beneficiary or beneficiaries of the income interest retained or created in such property, the number of Units so assigned being equal to the number obtained by dividing the fair market value of the property by $10.00.

B. ALLOCATION OF UNITS UPON SUBSEQUENT DONATIONS ON A DETERMINATION DATE. The term "determination date" means each day within the taxable year of the Fund on which a valuation is made of the property in the Fund. The property in the Fund shall be valued on January 1 of each year and on the last business day of each month during the year (including January) except for the month of December.

On each transfer of property by a donor on a determination date (subsequent to the initial donations referred to in paragraph A hereof), one or more Units shall be assigned to the beneficiary or beneficiaries of the income interest retained or created in such property based on the fair market value of the property on such determination date. The number of Units assigned shall equal the number obtained by dividing the fair market value of the property by the fair market value of a Unit in the Fund on such determination date. The fair market value of a Unit in the Fund shall be determined by dividing the fair market value of all property in the Fund on such determination date by the number of Units then in the Fund. The computation provided for in the preceding sentence shall be made after the redemption of Units as provided for in Article VI hereof and after the distribution of income from the Fund as provided in Article V hereof, and before adding to the Fund the property with which the new Units are being acquired. Although the value of each Unit of participation will fluctuate with each new transfer of property to the Fund in relation to the appreciation or depreciation of the fair market value of the property in the Fund, all units in the Fund will always have equal value.

C. TRANSFERS BETWEEN DETERMINATION DATES. If a transfer of property to the Fund occurs on other than a determination date, the number of Units assigned as a result of such donation shall be determined by using the fair market value of the property in the Fund on the determination date immediately preceding the date of transfer (determined as set forth in Article III B hereof and without regard to the property so transferred), subject, however, to appropriate adjustment on the next succeeding determination date to take account of any changes in the fair market value of the property in the Fund between the preceding determination date and the date of transfer. Such adjustments shall be made in any reasonable method chosen by the Trustee in its discretion, including the use of a method whereby the fair market value of the property in the Fund at the time of the transfer is deemed to be the average of the fair market values of the property in the Fund on the determination dates immediately preceding and succeeding the date of transfer. For purposes of determining such average any property transferred to the Fund between such preceding and succeeding dates, or on such succeeding date, shall be excluded. Notwithstanding anything herein to the contrary, the Trustee shall not use any method for making the adjustments provided for herein that has not previously been approved by the Internal Revenue Service.

D. VALUATION. The Trustee shall have the discretion to choose the method for determining fair market value and the time in the business day for valuation when required for computations set out herein. Such discretion shall be exercised in accordance with customary fiduciary accounting practices and in accordance with any United States Treasury regulations and Internal Revenue Service rulings, procedures, and guidelines governing pooled income funds.

ARTICLE IV

Determination of Income

A. The determination by the Trustee of all matters with respect to what shall constitute principal of the trust estate, gross income therefrom, and net income distributable under the terms of the Trust shall be governed by the provisions of the Principal and Income Law of the State of California as they may from time to time exist, except as any of such matters may otherwise be provided for herein. In the event and to the extent that any of such matters relating to what constitutes principal and income of the trust estate is not provided for either herein or in said Principal and Income Law, the Trustee shall have full power and authority to determine such matter in the Trustee's discretion. The Trustee may rely upon the statement of the paying corporation as to whether dividends are paid from profits or earnings or are a return of capital, and as to any other fact relevant hereunder concerning the source or character of dividends or distributions of corporate assets.

B. The Trustee shall make an allowance to corpus, in accordance with generally accepted accounting principles, from income received on account of any depreciable or depletable asset held in the trust.

C. Notwithstanding any contrary provisions in this instrument, the Trustee shall treat all dividends which are designated by the corporation declaring such dividend as a return of capital, and all dividends of regulated investment companies which represent a distribution of capital gains realized from the sale of assets owned by such companies, as principal of the trust estate.

D. Notwithstanding any contrary provisions herein, the Trustee shall treat all gains from the sale of capital assets as principal of the trust estate.

ARTICLE V

Distribution of Income

A. The Trustee shall make income payments monthly to each beneficiary to whom Units have been assigned; provided, however, that the final income payment for each taxable year may be made at any time within 65 days of the close of such taxable year. Any such payment made after the close of such taxable year shall be treated as paid on the last day of the taxable year. Units outstanding for less than a full month shall receive income by appropriately taking into consideration the period of time such Units are outstanding. Distributable income shall be computed on the last business day of each month.

B. If a beneficiary holding Units shall die on or prior to any determination date, the income interest of such beneficiary shall terminate as of the determination date preceding the date of death and the income such beneficiary would have been entitled to receive pursuant to paragraph A of this Article V had he been living on the day after the determination date coinciding with or following death shall be distributed:

1. To a successive life income beneficiary if such beneficiary is then entitled to succeed to the income interest; or

2. If no such successive life income beneficiary exists, to Pomona as a portion of its remainder interest in the Fund.

Article VI
Severance of Property from Fund for Remainderman

At such time as the beneficiaries entitled to income from a Unit of the Fund shall be deceased, that Unit shall vest in Pomona as Remainderman as of such date of death. On the coinciding or next succeeding determination date after death occurs, the Trustee, after determining the Unit value, shall distribute to the Remainderman money or other assets equal in value to the value of all such vested Units together with any income allocated thereto as provided in Article V B2 above. The Unit value shall be determined by dividing the total number of Units (before any redemption of Units) into the value of the Fund on the determination date. After the date of such distribution, such assets shall not be commingled with properties of the Fund but, in the discretion of the Trustee, such assets may be invested or reinvested jointly with assets in the Fund to the extent such investment is permissible under Section 642 (c) (5) of the Code.

Article VII
Powers of the Trustee

A. To carry out the purposes of this trust, and subject to any limitations herein expressed, the Trustee is vested with the following powers until final distribution in addition to any now or hereafter conferred by law affecting the trust or trust estate. In exercising such powers, the Trustee shall act in a manner which is reasonable and equitable in view of the interests of income and principal beneficiaries, and in the manner in which men of ordinary prudence, diligence, discretion, and judgment would act in the management of their own affairs.

1. To retain any property received at the inception of the trust or at any other time, whether or not such property is property in which the Trustee is personally interested or in which the Trustee owns an undivided interest in any other trust capacity.

2. To continue or participate in the operation of any business or other enterprise at the risk of the trust estate and not at the risk of the Trustee, and to effect incorporation, dissolution, or other change in the form of the organization of the business or enterprise.

3. To invest and reinvest principal, and income if accumulated, in such securities and properties as the Trustee may deem advisable, not in regard to speculation, but in regard to the permanent disposition of the trust funds, considering the probable income as well as the probable safety of the capital. Within the limitations of the foregoing standard, the Trustee is authorized to acquire, for cash or on credit, every kind of property, real, personal, or mixed, and every

kind of investment, specifically including, but not by way of limitation, corporate or governmental obligations of every kind (except as provided in paragraph C of Article I hereof), stocks, preferred or common, securities of any regulated investment trust, and property in which the Trustee owns an undivided interest in any other trust capacity.

4. To deposit trust funds in commercial, savings, or savings and loan accounts, subject to the usual restrictions upon withdrawal in effect at that time.

5. To dispose of an asset, for cash or on credit, at public or private sale, and in connection with any sale or disposition, to give such warranties and indemnifications as the Trustee shall determine; to manage, develop, improve, exchange, partition, change the character of, or abandon a trust asset or any interest therein.

6. To borrow money for any trust purpose upon such terms and conditions as may be determined by the Trustee, and to obligate the trust estate for the repayment thereof; to encumber the trust estate or any part thereof by mortgage, deed of trust, pledge or otherwise, for a term within or extending beyond the term of the trust.

7. To make ordinary or extraordinary repairs or alterations in building or other structures, to demolish any improvements, to raze existing or erect new party walls or buildings.

8. To subdivide land; to make or obtain the vacation of plats and adjust boundaries; to adjust differences in valuation on exchange or partition by giving or receiving consideration; to dedicate land or easements in land to public use with or without consideration.

9. To enter for any purpose into a lease as lessor or lessee with or without option to purchase or renew for a term within or extending beyond the term of the trust; to amend or extend existing leases.

10. To enter into a lease or arrangement for exploration and removal of minerals or other natural resources or enter into pooling or unitization agreements.

11. To grant options and rights of first refusal involving the sale or lease of any trust asset, or to acquire options and rights of first refusal for the purchase or lease of any asset.

12. To create restrictions, easements, and other servitudes, with or without consideration.

13. To loan or reloan the trust estate, or any part thereof, as the Trustee shall determine.

14. To have, respecting securities, all the rights, powers, and privileges of an owner, including, without limiting the foregoing, the power to vote, give general or limited proxies, pay calls, assessments, and other sums as the Trustee shall determine; to assent to corporate

sales or other acts; to participate in voting trusts, pooling agreements, foreclosures, reorganizations, consolidations, mergers, and liquidations, and in connection therewith to give such warranties and indemnifications as the Trustee shall determine and to deposit securities with and transfer title to any protective or other committee under such terms as the Trustee shall determine; to exchange, exercise, or sell stock subscription or conversion rights; to accept and retain as an investment hereunder any securities received through the exercise of any of the foregoing powers.

15. To hold securities or other property in the name of the Trustee, in the name of a nominee of the Trustee, or in the name of a custodian (or its nominee) selected by the Trustee, with or without disclosure of this trust, the Trustee being responsible for the acts of such custodian or nominee affecting such property.

16. To carry such insurance as the Trustee shall determine.

17. To advance money for the protection of the trust, and for all expenses, losses, and liabilities sustained in the administration of the trust or because of the holding or ownership of any trust assets, for which advances with any interest the Trustee has a lien on the trust assets as against the beneficiary.

18. To pay or contest any claim; to settle a claim by or against the trust by compromise, arbitration, or otherwise; and to release, in whole or in part, any claim belonging to the trust to the extent that the claim is uncollectible.

19. To prosecute or defend actions, claims, or proceedings for the protection of trust assets and of the Trustee in the performance of its duties.

20. To employ persons, corporations, or associations, including attorneys, auditors, investment advisers, or agents, even if they are associated with the Trustee, to advise or assist the Trustee in the performance of its administrative duties; to act without independent investigation upon their recommendations; and instead of acting personally, to employ one or more custodians or agents to perform any ministerial act of administration.

21. To pay any expense for the management, collection, or protection of the trust estate, and any taxes or assessments that may be levied upon the trust estate or the income thereof.

22. To set up reserves out of income for the payment of taxes, assessments, insurance, repairs, fees, and other expenses of the trust; to determine in the exercise of good trust management whether a reserve for depreciation or depletion is necessary with regard to depreciating or depletable assets, and if such a reserve is necessary to establish such a reserve; to determine, in accordance with Article

IV hereof, which funds shall be classified as income or principal and which expenses shall be chargeable to income or principal.

23. To execute and deliver all instruments which will accomplish or facilitate the exercise of the powers vested in the Trustee.

24. A material purpose in establishing this trust is to obtain for donors the charitable deduction allowable pursuant to the provisions of the Code or other similar statute in force from time to time. The Trustee is, therefore, expressly authorized to enter into any and all agreements with the Internal Revenue Service or any other governmental body or official or to execute, from time to time, any declarations of policy or disclaimers restricting the discretion given it in order to preserve the charitable deduction provided for herein. Moreover, the Trustee shall exercise all powers and discretion only in a manner consistent with the allowance of all federal charitable tax deductions to which donors may otherwise be entitled under the provisions of the Code.

B. Notwithstanding any other provisions in this instrument to the contrary, this trust is prohibited from engaging in any act of "self-dealing" (as such term is defined in Section 4941(d) of the Code), and from making any "taxable expenditure" (as such term is defined in Section 4945(d) of the Code), except that "self-dealing" and "taxable expenditure" shall not include payments expressly required by Articles V and VI above. References in this paragraph to sections of the Code shall also be deemed to apply to any corresponding or substitute provisions that may exist from time to time.

ARTICLE VIII
Notice of Termination of Life Interest

Until the Trustee shall receive written notice of any death, the Trustee shall incur no liability to persons whose interests may have been affected by such death, for disbursements made by the Trustee in good faith.

ARTICLE IX
Revocation, Amendment, and Termination

This trust shall be irrevocable and not subject to amendment except as shall be necessary to conform it to any requirement of the law relating to pooled income funds, as defined in Section 642(c)(5) of the Code, as amended and interpreted by pronouncements of the Internal Revenue Service. Donors, by transferring property to the Fund subject to the above power of amendment, agree that the Trustee is authorized without notice to the donor or any beneficiary to amend this trust so as to conform it to applicable requirements imposed on pooled income funds. This trust shall terminate at such time as all Units have vested in the remainderman.

Article X
Method for Transfer of Property Into Fund

This trust shall come into existence at such time as Units in the Fund are issued to the first donor or donors of property to the Fund. Units in the Fund shall be issued to donors pursuant to written agreements referring to this trust, which agreements together with this trust shall constitute the governing instrument with respect to each gift of property. Such agreement shall not amend or affect the provisions of this trust but shall supplement it by setting forth the value of property transferred by donor, the number of Units to which the donor is entitled, the date upon which the transfer is made, and the designation of the beneficiary or beneficiaries who shall be entitled to income from the Fund.

Article XI
General

A. This trust has been created by the Trustee in the State of California, and its validity, construction, and all rights under it shall be governed by the laws of that state.

B. The Trustee shall not receive any compensation for its services in administering this trust.

C. In the event the Trustee is required to distribute any moneys hereunder to an incompetent person, each such distribution may, at the sole discretion of the Trustee, be made to such beneficiary without the intervention of a guardian or a conservator; or the Trustee may expend the money for the benefit of such beneficiary, or the Trustee may distribute to a guardian or a conservator. The Trustee shall not be required to see to the application of any such payments so made to any of said persons, but such payees' receipts therefor shall be full discharge to the Trustee.

Executed at Claremont, California, this _____ day of _____, effective _____.

POMONA COLLEGE

By _____
   Treasurer

By _____
   Assistant Treasurer

Gift Annuity Agreement

WHEREAS, _____ and _____,
husband and wife, of _____, _____
have given to POMONA COLLEGE, a California nonprofit corporation having its office and principal place of business in the City of Claremont, County of Los Angeles, State of California, the following described property:

Cash in the amount of $_____

upon the sole condition that, in consideration of said gift, Pomona College shall pay, as an annuity, the sum of $_____ per annum as hereinafter provided:

NOW, THEREFORE, Pomona College, acting under authority of its Board of Trustees, and in consideration of the transfer to it of said property, hereby covenants and agrees to pay the said sum of $_____ per annum to said _____ and _____, during their lifetime, and upon the death of either of them, then to the survivor for life, such payments to be made at the Business Office of said Corporation in Claremont, California, in _____ payments of $_____ each commencing on the _____ day of _____, ____, and ending with the regular payment next preceding the death of the survivor of _____ and _____.
_____ reserves a special power to appoint to Pomona College one-half of the annuity payments payable after his death, and _____ reserves a special power to appoint to Pomona College one-half of the annuity payments payable after her death. Each such power may be exercised only by a written instrument filed with Pomona College.

The age of _____ at his nearest birthday is _____ years. The age of _____ at her nearest birthday is _____ years.

The reasonably commensurate value, as of the date of this

Agreement and as defined by Chapter 12 of Part 2 of Division 2 of the Insurance Code of the State of California, of the benefits hereby created, is $_____.

IN WITNESS WHEREOF, Pomona College has hereunto caused to be subscribed and affixed its corporate name and seal and this obligation to be executed by its duly authorized officers this _____ day of _____, _____.

POMONA COLLEGE

By _____
                    Treasurer

By _____
              Assistant Treasurer

Glossary

(see also Definition of Terms in Ernst & Whinney Report, pp. 00–00)

ACKNOWLEDGMENT: Confirmation of receipt of a gift or service. Usually contains an expression of gratitude to donor.

ALUMNI FUND: The organized effort by most educational institutions to secure gifts on an annual basis from their own alumni, including publicly as well as privately supported colleges, universities, and preparatory schools.

ANNUAL FUND: Any organized effort by a *nonprofit* institution or program to secure gifts on an annual basis, either by mail or through direct solicitation, or both. Also frequently called Annual Appeal or Annual Giving Program.

ANNUITANT: An individual who receives or who is scheduled to receive annuity payments.

ANNUITY (CHARITABLE): A gift to a nonprofit institution in return for a contract to pay donor and/or another annuitant an annual fixed amount for life. The amount to be paid is normally determined from actuarial rate tables based on age(s) of the annuitant(s) and may include other factors as agreed upon by either of the parties making the contract.

A deferred gift annuity is one where the payments to the donor will not begin until at least one year after the annuity has been purchased.

APPRECIATED SECURITIES GIFT: A gift of securities with a market value in excess of the donor's cost or basis.

Sources for this Glossary include a study sponsored by the American Association of Fund Raising Counsel, Inc., National Society of Fund Raisers, Inc., National Association for Hospital Development; Compilation by Douglas N. Allinger, *Fundraising Management* (August 1980), p. 18.

The gift value of a security which is traded on an exchange or in the over-the-counter market is established by the mean between the high and low prices on the date it is transferred to the nonprofit institution. The transfer date is the date on which the securities are personally delivered to the institution, or the postmarked date on which the securities and executed stock power are mailed, or the date the donor contacts his or her broker ordering the transfer of the securities or assets to the charitable organization.

BASIS OF PROPERTY: The value used to determine gain or loss for income tax purposes. The basis may be cost or a different amount, depending on the law affecting the transaction.

BENEFACTOR: One who makes a major gift to an institution or agency; also, an arbitrary classification of contributors whose gifts are above a certain level, which is calculated to single them out as a group and to stimulate similar giving by others.

BENEFICIARY: One who receives income from a trust; also one who benefits from the actions of another as to be the recipient of something of value such as life insurance proceeds or a bequest, also, "Legatee" and "Devisee." (See also Bequest.)

BEQUEST: A gift made through a will of personal and/or real property, such as cash, land, securities, or other assets. Where cash or securities are given, the term "Legacy" is used to describe a bequest. Where real estate is given, the term "Devise" is used to describe a bequest.

BOOK VALUE: The actual or net value of an asset at the time of acquisition computed according to standard accounting practices.

BUDGET: A detailed breakdown of the estimated costs and expenses of a project or program.

CAMPAIGN: An organized effort to raise funds for a nonprofit organization for designated purposes or periods of time.

CAPITAL CAMPAIGN: A campaign to raise substantial funds for a nonprofit organization to finance major needs demanding extensive capital.

CAPITAL GAIN: Profit resulting from the sale or other disposition of a capital asset (e.g., stocks, bonds, real estate not held for sale in the ordinary course of business).

A profit from an asset held 12 months or more is considered a long-term capital gain, less than 12 months a short-term gain, for Federal tax purposes. State laws may differ.

CASE: The combination of reasons advanced by a charitable institution in justification of its appeal for support.

CHARITABLE CONTRIBUTION: A donation of anything having value to a charitable institution.

CHARITABLE CONTRIBUTION DEDUCTION: An allowable adjustment to income, gift, or estate tax liability by statute for the value (or a part thereof) of any gift or bequest to a recognized charity.

CHARITABLE GIFT ANNUITY: A contractual agreement between a charitable institution and a donor whereby donor contributes cash or assets of a determinable value to the institution in return for a guaranteed payment of a fixed amount for life.

CHARITABLE INSTITUTION: An institution or agency that operates on a nonprofit basis for the public good and which qualifies as tax-exempt under the definitions in the Federal Internal Revenue Code.

CHARITABLE REMAINDER ANNUITY TRUST: A contractual agreement creating a trust between a charitable institution (or another designated trustee) and a donor who contributes cash or securities or property to the institution which, in turn, agrees to pay donor and/or named beneficiaries a fixed amount annually of not less than 5% of the initial value of the trust. Payments are for life of donor or lives of other named beneficiaries. Remainder goes to the charitable institution upon death of donor and other named beneficiaries. No additional contributions to trust are permitted. No liability for payment extends beyond the trust assets.

CHARITABLE REMAINDER POOLED INCOME FUND: A number of separate irrevocable life income agreements which are pooled and commingled for investment and management purposes. The donor or his designees owns a pro rata share of the pool and receives an annual income for his or her lifetime that represents his or her pro rata share of the overall pool income. Upon the death of the beneficiary, the value of his or her pro rata share is transferable to the designated charitable institution.

CHARITABLE REMAINDER TRUST: A trust providing that the remainder be paid over to charity.

CHARITABLE REMAINDER UNITRUST: A contractural agreement creating a trust between a charitable institution (or another designated trustee) and a donor who contributes cash or securities or property to the institution which, in turn, agrees to pay donor and/or other named beneficiaries a fixed amount annually equal to at least 5% of the trust as valued annually or may provide for the payment of income only if the actual income is less than the stated percentage. Remainder goes to the charitable institution upon death of donor and other named beneficiaries. Additional contributions to trust are permitted. No liability for payment extends beyond the trust assets.

CODICIL: An addition to a will, which may modify, add to, subtract from, qualify, alter, or revoke provisions in the will. The codicil is a separate document. It is signed with the same formalities as a will and can itself be changed, revoked, canceled, or destroyed at any time.

COMMITMENT (CHARITABLE): The promise to provide a charitable organization with something of value, generally within a specified time. A commitment can take the form of a written pledge, a letter of intent, a testamentary document, or a similar communication.

CONSTITUENCY: A category of donors and prospective donors, such as alumni, parents, and in a broader sense, individuals, corporations, and foundations.

CORPUS: The principal or capital, as distinguished from the interest or income, of a fund, estate, investment, or the like.

CULTIVATION: The process of gradually developing the interest of an important prospective contributor through exposure to institutional activities, people, needs, and plans to the point where he may consider a major gift.

CURRENT GIVING: Gifts toward current operations of an institution.

DEFERRED GIFTS: A gift arrangement where a charity's realization of use of the gift assets is postponed. Examples include Life Income Gifts, Annuity Trusts, Unitrusts, Pooled Income Funds, Charitable Gift Annuities, Life Insurance, and Testamentary Commitments.

DEFERRED GIVING PROGRAM: An organized effort by an institution to secure long-term commitments through various forms of deferred gifts.

DEFERRED OR PLANNED GIFT: A commitment or gift established legally during the donor's lifetime, but whose principal benefits do not accrue to the recipient until some future time, usually at the death of the donor. This term is usually applied to any arrangement whereby money or property is irrevocably (except for testamentary commitments) set aside for future receipt by a nonprofit organization. Annuities, trusts, and testamentary commitments are all generally referred to as deferred gifts. Such gifts can also be established by will or codicil.

DEVELOPMENT: A term used since the mid-1940s to define the total process of institutional fundraising, frequently inclusive of public relations and alumni affairs. (See also Fundraising)

DEVELOPMENT OFFICE: The organized division of an institution responsible for all facets of its development program.

DEVELOPMENT PROGRAM: Total development efforts and operations of a nonprofit organization, as carried out by the development office.

DEVELOPMENT STAFF: All paid personnel involved in an institutional development program.

DONOR FINANCIAL PLANNING: The efforts some nonprofit institutions are making to obtain philanthropic support from individuals through the presentation of gift proposals based upon the application of sound estate planning principles.

ESTATE: Total assets of a deceased person.

FAIR MARKET VALUE: A value generally defined as the amount that a willing purchaser would pay in a normal market. The responsibility for determining this value is generally left to the donor. (See also Appreciated Securities Gift for valuation rules.)

Gifts of personal property other than securities and other items for which there is an *established* market are often valued in a way which is acceptable to the IRS for purposes of tax deductibility using more than one documented appraisal from recognized authorities.

FIDUCIARY: A person charged with the duty of trust on behalf of a beneficiary. Executors and trustees are fiduciaries.

FRIENDS: A category of donors and prospective donors; also an organized group which supports a specified project, such as "Friends of the Library" or "Friends of Art," etc.

FUNDRAISING: Generic term for the seeking of gifts from various sources. (See also Development.)

GIFT PROCESSING: The procedure by which gifts are received, recorded, transmitted for deposit, receipted, and acknowleged, all in an orderly sequence and in keeping with established accounting procedures.

GIFT RECORDS: The current and cumulative records of contributions variously maintained on cards, in files, or on a computer system.

INTER VIVOS TRANSFERS: Transfers of property made during one's lifetime as opposed to testamentary disposition made under a person's will.

JOINT AND SURVIVOR ANNUITY: An annuity from which one spouse (or another person) receives the stated payments during his or her life, and upon his or her death, the payments continue for the benefit of the surviving spouse (or another person).

LIFE ESTATE: Donor conveys residence, ranch, or farm to a charitable institution and retains right for him and his wife, or named beneficiary, to live there for life.

LIFE INCOME GIFTS: Irrevocable gifts of cash and/or securities and/or real estate to a nonprofit institution (or other designated trustee), with the donor or his designees receiving income or payments from the donated assets through an annuity or trust arrangement.

LIFE INTEREST: An interest or claim that does not amount to ownership and which is held only for the duration of the life of the person to whom the interest is given or for the duration of the life of another person. An interest in property for life.

NONPROFIT INSTITUTION: A private or public institution that provides services of benefit to mankind without profit and thus can qualify as a charitable institution under the provisions of the U.S. Internal Revenue Code.

OUTRIGHT GIFT: A present gift made to an institution the use of which is immediately available.

PHILANTHROPY: The philosophy and practice of supporting through financial and other contributions, development programs and campaigns conducted by charitable institutions. Acts of charity.

PLANNED GIFTS: see Deferred Gifts

PLEDGE: A promise to pay or provide a specified charitable commitment within a specified period of time. (See also Commitment.)

PROPOSAL: A carefully prepared written request for a gift or grant; also known as "presentation."

PROSPECT: The target of all fundraising, any logical source of support, whether individual, corporation, organization, government at all levels, or foundation; with emphasis on the logicality of support.

RECORDS: Collective term for all files and lists pertaining to donors, nondonors, prospects, gift records, and miscellaneous records as maintained by a development office.

REMAINDER: Property remaining in a trust at the time it terminates or at the end of a life estate.

REMAINDER INTEREST: The rights one holds in the remainder of a trust, or other property.

REMAINDERMAN: The individual(s) and/or institution(s) entitled to receive the principal upon termination of a trust.

RESTRICTED GIFT: A gift for a specified purpose.

SOLICITATION: The process of asking for a charitable contribution.

SUPPORT SERVICES: Technical aspects of a development program or fundraising campaign, which deal with such areas as prospect research, mailings, gift processing, list preparation, and clerical operations generally.

TAX BENEFITS: Savings in income, gift, and estate taxes (federal, state, county, city, etc.) brought about by carefully planned giving to charitable institutions.

TESTAMENTARY: Provisions for after-death disposition of assets as set forth in a will.

TESTAMENTARY GIFT: A charitable gift designated in a will which becomes effective upon the death of the testator.

TESTAMENTARY TRUST: A trust contained wholly within the will of a deceased person. Effective only after death.

TRUST: A set of written instructions to a trustee with management authority over the trust property (also called Corpus, Res, Capital, or Principal) which is to be managed exclusively for the benefit of a named beneficiary.

TRUST DEED OR INDENTURE: The formal document or instrument under which a trust is created.

TRUSTEE: Person or corporation with trust powers given management authority over property by its former owner. Also a person elected or appointed to serve on a governing board or other decision-making body of a charitable institution.

UNRESTRICTED GIFT: A gift made unconditionally, the reverse of a restricted gift.

VEST: To confer ownership of property or a right to property upon a person in whole or in part. To give a person or organization an immediate fixed right of present or future enjoyment of property.

WILL(S): The legal declaration of a person's intentions as to the disposal of his or her estate after death. A written instrument legally executed by which a person makes disposition of his or her property to take effect after death.

holographic will: A will entirely written and signed by the testator or maker in his or her own hand.

nuncupative will: An oral will made by a person in his last illness or extremity before witnesses, often not honored in a court of law.

pour-over will: A will whereby assets controlled by the will are directed to be poured-over into a preexistent trust.

reciprocal wills: Wills made by two persons in which they leave everything to each other.

Bibliography

AAFRC. *Giving U.S.A.* (an annual yearbook on philanthropy). New York: American Association of Fund Raising Counsel, 1977.

Andrews, Frank Emerson. *Attitudes Toward Giving.* New York: Russell Sage Foundation, 1953.

Andrews, Frank Emerson. *Philanthropic Giving.* New York: Russell Sage Foundation, 1950.

Barton, D. W., Jr., ed. *New Directions for Higher Education,* no. 21, San Francisco: Jossey-Bass, 1978.

Beeman, A. L. "No Future Without Risk." *CASE Current* (December 1976), 2(11):4–7.

Berry, L. L. and B. H. Allen, "Marketing's Crucial Role for Institutions of Higher Education." *Atlanta Economic Review* (1977), 27(4):24–31.

Brakeley, George A., Jr. "Deferred Gifts & Bequests." *Tested Ways to Successful Fundraising.* New York: Amacom, 1980, 136–144.

Brannon, Gerard M. "Alternative Approaches to Encouraging Philanthropic Activities." Reprinted from the Research Papers of the Filer Commission. Washington, D.C.: GPO, 1977.

Bucklin, L. W. "Deferred Giving." In A. W. Rowland, ed., *Handbook of Institutional Advancement.* San Francisco: Jossey-Bass, 1977.

Butners, Astrida and Norman Buntaine. *Motivations for Charitable Giving: A Reference Guide.* Washington, D.C.: The 501(c) (3) Group, 1973.

Carnegie Commission on Higher Education. *Institutions in Transition: A Profile of Change in Higher Education.* New York: McGraw-Hill, 1971.

Cary, William L. and Craig B. Bright. *The Development Law of Endowment Funds: "The Law and the Lore" Revisited.* New York: Ford Foundation, 1974.

Cassell, W. C., ed. *Deferred Giving Programs: Administration and Promotion.* Washington, D.C. American Alumni Council, 1972.

Connell, James E. "Marry Capital Giving Cycle with Deferred Giving Cycle." *Fund Raising Management* (May 1980). Garden City, N.Y.: Hoke Communications.

CASE. "Planned Giving Ideas." *The Best of CASE Currents*. Washington, D.C.: Council for Advancement and Support of Education, 1979.

CASE. "Planned Giving: Part I." *CASE Currents*, Washington, D.C.: Council for Advancement and Support of Education, November 1979.

CASE. *Deferred Giving Programs: Administration and Promotion.* Washington, D.C.: Council for Advancement and Support of Education, 1972.

CASE. *Guide to the Administration of Charitable Remainder Trusts.* 3d ed. Washington, D.C.: Council for Advancement and Support of Education, 1974.

COFHE. *A Comparative Study of Development and University Relations at Twenty-Five Colleges and Universities.* Washington, D.C.: Consortium on Financing Higher Education, 1976.

Curti, Merle Eugene and Roderick Nash, *Philanthropy in the Shaping of American Higher Education.* New Brunswick, N.J.: Rutgers University Press, 1965.

Cutlip, S. M. *Fundraising in the United States: Its Role in America's Philanthropy.* New Brunswick, N.J.: Rutgers University Press, 1965.

Desmond, Richard L. *Higher Education and Tax-Motivated Giving.* Washington, D.C.: American College Public Relations Association, 1967.

Drucker, Peter F. *The Effective Executive.* New York: Harper & Row, 1967.

Dunseth, W. B. *An Introduction to Annuity, Life Income, and Bequest Programs.* Washington, D.C.: Council for the Advancement and Support of Education, 1978.

Filer Commission on Private Philanthropy and Public Needs. *Giving in America: Toward a Stronger Voluntary Sector.* Washington, D.C.: GPO, 1975.

Fink, N. S. "1977: Rites of Passage—From the Tripod to the Waterbed of Philanthropy." *CASE Currents* (July 1977).

FRI. *Bequest Program Handbook.* Plymouth Meeting, Pa.: Fund Raising Institute, 1970.

FRI. *Deferred-Giving Handbook.* Ambler, Pa.: Fund Raising Institute, 1977.

Friday Report. Hoke Communications, Garden City, N.Y. Weekly.

FRI Newsletter. Fund Raising Institute, Plymouth Meeting, Pa. Monthly.

FRM Weekly. Fund raising management magazine. Garden City, N.Y.

Fulmer, V. A. "Cost/Benefit Analysis in Fund Raising." *Harvard Business Review* (March–April 1973), pp. 103–110.

Fund Raising Management. Garden City, N.Y.: Hoke Communications. Bi-monthly.

Fund Raising Management Special Issue. "Is There a Planned Giving in Your Future." Garden City, N.Y.: Hoke Communications.

Giving USA. American Association of Fund-Raising Counsel, 1980. New York.

Giving USA and *The Bulletin.* American Association of Fund-Raising Counsel, New York. 11 Bulletins and annual report.

Grimes, Arthur Jack. "The Fund Raising Percent as a Quantitative Standard for Regulation of Public Charities with Particular Emphasis on Voluntary Health and Welfare Organizations." Reprinted from the Research Papers of the Filer Commission. Washington, D.C.: GPO, 1977.

Harris, S. E. *Higher Education: Resources and Finance.* New York: McGraw-Hill, 1962.

Heemann, Warren, ed. *Analyzing the Cost Effectiveness of Fund Raising.* San Francisco: Jossey-Bass, 1979.

Hopkins, Bruce R. and John Holt Meyers. *The Law of Tax-Exempt Organizations.* Washington, D.C.: Learner Law Book Co., 1975.

Hunter, T. Willard. *The Tax Climate for Philanthropy.* Washington, D.C. American College Public Relations Association, 1968.

Isackes, Charles F. and David W. Clark. *The Case for Deferred Giving.* The American Alumni Council, 1966.

Kotler, P. *Marketing for Non-Profit Organizations.* Prentice-Hall, 1975.

Kramer, Albert H. "The Role of Foundations in Broadcasting and Cable Communications Policy Development." Reprinted from the Research Papers of the Filer Commission. Washington, D.C.: GPO, 1977.

Leslie, J. W. *Focus on Understanding and Support: A Study in College Management.* Washington, D.C.: American College Public Relations Association, 1969.

Leslie, J. W. *Institutional Advancement Management Survey.* Washington, D.C.: Institutional Advancement Consultants, 1977.

Leslie, J. W. *Seeking the Competitive Dollar: College Management in the Seventies.* Washington, D.C.: American College Public Relations Association, 1971.

Levy, Reynold and Waldemar A. Nielsen. "An Agenda for the Future." Reprinted from the Research Papers of the Filer Commission on Private Philanthropy and Public Needs. Washington, D.C.: GPO, 1977.

Lyon, E. W. The History of Pomona College 1887–1969. Claremont, Calif.: Castle Press, 1977.

Main, Jeremy. "Gifts That Help the Giver Too." Money Magazine (December 1979).

Mason, Alpheus T. Brandeis: A Free Man's Life. New York: Viking, 1946.

Nelson, Charles A. "Does Management by Objectives Make Sense for Colleges and Universities?" Management Focus (March/April 1979), pp. 8–11. New York: Peat, Marwick, Mitchell & Co.

Nelson, Ralph L. "Private Giving in the American Economy: 1960–1972." Reprinted from the Research Papers of the Filer Commission, 1977.

Non-Profit Organization Tax Letter. Bethesda, Md.: Organization Management. 18 issues per year.

NAF. The Deferred Gifts Program II, 1974–1980. Saint Paul, Minn.: Northwest Area Foundation, 1980.

NAF. The Deferred Gifts Program, Future Funding for Private Colleges. Saint Paul, Minn.: Northwest Area Foundation, 1978.

Philanthropic Digest. New York: Brakeley, John Price Jones. 10 issues per year.

Philanthropy Monthly. Danbury, Conn. Monthly.

Philanthropy Monthly. How to Raise Charitable Funds: A Special Section (September 1979), Danbury, Conn.

PTI. Charitable Contributions and Estate Planning, Tax Reform Act of 1976. Old Greenwich, Conn.: Philanthropy Tax Institute, 1976.

Rourke, F. and G. Brooks. The Managerial Revolution in Higher Education. Baltimore, Md.: Johns Hopkins University Press, 1966.

Sacks, Albert M. "The Role of Philanthropy: An Institutional View." Virginia Law Review (April 1960), vol. 46.

Schooler, Dean, Jr. "Rethinking & Remaking the Nonprofit Sector." Foundation News (January-February 1978), pp. 17–21.

Schwartz, J. J. "Tax Legislation, Regulation of Charitable Organizations." Fund Raising Management (January-February 1978), pp. 18–23.

Seymour, Harold J. Designs for Fund Raising. New York: McGraw-Hill, 1966.

Sharpe, Robert F. *The Planned Giving Idea Book.* New York: Thomas Nelson, 1978.

Smallwood, S. J. and W. C. Levis. "The Realities of Fund-Raising Costs and Accountability." *The Philanthropy Monthly* (September 1977), pp. 15–23.

Taxes for Fundraisers. Larchmont, N.Y.: J. K. Lasser Tax Institute. Monthly.

Taxwise Giving. *Deferred Giving,* vols. 1 and 2. Conrad Teitell, ed. Old Greenwich, Conn.: Taxwise Giving, 1977.

Taxwise Giving. Conrad Teitell, ed. Old Greenwich, Conn. Monthly.

Taylor, Bernard P. "The Lifetime Gift Deferred." *Guide to Creative Giving.* South Plainfield, N.J.: Groupwork Today, 1980.

The 501(c) (3) Group. *Motivation for Charitable Giving: A Reference Guide.* Washington, D.C.: The 501(c) (3) Group.

TIA. *Tax Impacts on Philanthropy.* Princeton, N.J.: Tax Institute of America.

Tideman, Nicolaus T. "Employment and Earnings in the Non-Profit Charitable Sector." Reprinted from the Research Papers of the Filer Commission, 1977.

Warner, Irving L. *The Art of Fund Raising.* New York: Harper and Row, 1975.

Weinstock, Harold. *Planning An Estate: A Guidebook of Principles and Techniques.* Colorado Springs, Shepards, 1977.

Williams, M. Jane. *Capital Ideas: Step by Step—How to Solicit Major Gifts from Private Sources.* 2d ed. Ambler, Pa.: Fund Raising Institute, 1975.

Index